How to Behave

by

L. M. RAINER

Pelekinesis

How to Behave by L. M. Rainer

ISBN 978-1-949790-36-8

eISBN 978-1-949790-37-5

Layout and book design by Mark Givens

Front cover painting "Kairouan (III)" by August Macke, 1914, watercolor, Westphalian State Museum for Art and Cultural History, Münster

First Pelekinesis Printing 2020

For information: Pelekinesis, 112 Harvard Ave #65, Claremont, CA 91711 USA

Library of Congress Cataloging-in-Publication Data

Names: Rainer, L. M., author.
Title: How to behave / by L.M. Rainer.
Description: Claremont, CA : Pelekinesis, 2020.
Identifiers: LCCN 2020006624 (print) | LCCN 2020006625 (ebook) | ISBN 9781949790368 (paperback) | ISBN 9781949790375 (ebook)
Subjects: LCSH: Etiquette. | Travel etiquette. | Etiquette in literature.
Classification: LCC BJ1853 .R26 2020 (print) | LCC BJ1853 (ebook) | DDC 395--dc23
LC record available at https://lccn.loc.gov/2020006624
LC ebook record available at https://lccn.loc.gov/2020006625

Pelekinesis
www.pelekinesis.com

HOW TO BEHAVE

by

L. M. RAINER

He who is virtuous is wise; and he who is wise is good; and he who is good is happy.

Boethius

CONTENTS

HOW TO BEHAVE

HOW TO BEHAVE IN THE MIDDLE EAST

HOW TO EXPAT

HOW TO TRAVEL

This book is dedicated to all those with panache who don't whine, steal, cheat, lie, or throw hissy fits; to those who are kind to teenagers, tip generously, fail to escalate verbal confrontations, and always leave the guest bedroom, kitchen, and other people's lives as clean as when they first found them. In other words, to those who behave well.

INTRODUCTION

THIS BOOK IS MEANT TO BE READ on the subway/metro as you go to work, so when you read a particularly funny line (of which there are a plethora of) you will snort in a particularly unattractive manner which will cause people around you to sigh in despair, roll their eyes, look disgruntled and subtly sift away from you, except for that one person on the train who glances over to see what you are reading because that person (CORRECTLY) knows that a snort of laughter while reading is always acceptable in places like subways, and that person is (WISELY) secretly wishing they were reading something amusing. This book might also be read in a café, preferably a non-chain café in an interesting location, say the top of the Eiffel Tower, Bismarck ND, Pitcairn Island, or Angkor Wat. Do not read this on a ski-lift or in a hot air balloon (look at the VIEW!). If you read this while sitting in the middle seat in a car or plane, laugh uproariously and refuse to let your seat mates read so much as one line, or the title of this book. And if you are reading this, please be assured that you are looking quite fabulous today, that shirt shows up the gold highlights in your eyes.

HOW TO BEHAVE

HOW TO BEHAVE

I BELIEVE THAT MOST PEOPLE LEAVE THEIR house wanting to be pleasant, but it often falls apart and suddenly someone is shrieking, "Where is my coffee?" And that someone is you. Not, by heavens, me. I am the one in the corner watching your unfortunate melt-down and wondering why your cherished aunt did not raise you better, then realizing that perhaps you did not have a cherished aunt to help prevent public melt-downs of the most unattractive kind. So I have stepped in. Here, my dear, in this one small book is all you need to survive, all the advice a cherished aunt can provide. The basic elements are self-control and self-knowledge, with many fabulous tips and artful advice. We, that is the royal we, start with the basics, reclaiming the word 'diva' from those who seek to cheapen in, then we move on to the fundamentals of life: cafes, spas, movies and coping with relatives. Once you have those mastered, you are allowed to move on to the next section of the book and leave the country.

THE HOW TO
BEHAVE EDICTS

How to Live in Harmony with your many selves, other selves, the world and the universe without being an over-weaning pain, sissy, troll, or drudge.

- Good intentions will not suffice. Act properly or stay home.

- Everything requires effort. Some stupid people understand this as "everything costs money." Don't think like that.

- Every action is complicated and requires much thought.

- Understand the difference between what you want (Russell Crowe on your personal Caribbean island) and what you are likely to be able to achieve (shaking his hand).

- There are stupid people, evil people, and stupid/evil people about.

- It is best not to be in the above three categories.

- Learn to differentiate between the above three categories.

- Harsh measure are occasionally called for (because of the trolls in the above three categories).

- Think about the kind of impression you want to make before you walk out the door, then make sure you create that impression.

- Revere your most important role-models, the three M's: Miss Manners, Martha, Miss Piggy.

Miss Manners is making a wonderful effort to improve you and has written many valuable books for your especial benefit. Buy them or check them out of your library and read them.

Martha Stewart is just heaven-sent; she is... what? What did you say? You don't like her? You're intimidated by her? You bought that book that's a spoof on her. Sigh. Fine, as you are a bowl of over-cooked spaghetti, I'm not wasting anther breath on you, go jog for all I care, out of my sight.

No, I refuse to listen to your drivel. You're wrong. Martha Stewart is a gift from the gods and if you are too blind to see that simple, essential fact, then...all right, all right, stop sniveling.

Look, it's important to have standards. It's important to care enough about special occasions and friends that you occasionally make an effort. And there's Martha to help you: a cornucopia of ideas on how to make Christmas festive, a picnic enchanting, Halloween exciting. Thank her. Bless her. But don't try to imitate every single decoration idea, don't try every recipe. From each issue of her magazine you might take one idea, the rest you just appreciate from a distance.

People who go on about being intimidated by Martha are those extremely boring type-A nitwits who made Law Review and know their golf handicap. Everyone, darling, has a golf handicap but no one should make a point of knowing it. These people are driven nuts by the fact that somewhere someone is actually creating something more perfect than them. Or else they have five kids, an old sofa, no time to write Christmas cards and they want to drag dear Martha down to their level of macaroni and cheese from a box.

Oh my Lord, people are stupid sometimes. Do you walk into the Uffizi and say, "Oh no, way overdone, let's get rid of some of these knick-knacks"? Embrace your boxed dinners, revel in your tin foil decorations, bless your mis-matched linens and then appreciate the fact that tonight for dinner Martha is having season-appropriate food on perfectly matched china with fabulous napkins and the most amazing and amusing table decorations.

Are we clear? You say another word about Martha and I will never speak to you again. But what about people who ridicule your attempts at design, cooking, and entertaining? This is just supposed to be the introduction, well, never mind, a short detour to help you cope with the unenlightened. First my dear, you must resolve to brush off attacks. If you let one little sneer ruin your day, then it's straight to a nunnery with you because you are too tender for the real world. Someone says, in that singular tone of voice, "Nice cushions." You smile and say, "Thank you." Yes, of course they meant it as a slam, but you can't go correcting every idiot who walks into your apartment. Let it go.

But a few too many comments, a few too many arched eyebrows and a lady is apt to get a trifle weary. Darling, pick your target. Don't go off the handle once you've reached your limit. Realize you are reaching your limit and pounce with a plan. Never on a person weaker than you. Think *Emma*, which you have of course read twice. Seeing the movie does not count. Remember when Emma, at the Box Hill picnic, makes fun of Miss Bates. Knightly rounds her royally for it and she deserved a good scolding. You get points taken away when you attempt to score them off a person younger, less knowing in the ways of the world, more awkward or more inept than you. Wait till the right person makes a comment on something, "Succotash-melon soup, how very last week" and then lie.

Oh no, you did not just say "Lying is wrong" because if you had said it, I would have to unilaterally declare you were switched at birth. I am not related to Puritans. Any comments? No, I thought not.

Now, you lie. With panache. With aplomb. With skill. "The soup," you smile sweetly, "Oh I had in France once and loved it." Don't say "I had it at the Louis XV," even if you did. Don't swan on about the places you've been. It's vulgar. But do let enough happen to slip out, casually in conversation.

What? You've never been outside the States? Oh dear me, get me a cold washcloth, my aching head. What were your parents thinking? No, no, don't apologize. Not your fault if your cherished mama could not arrange to have your born in Italy.

Back to the mission at hand: stopping my little diva to-be from being dissed. Your chocolate pie made with pre-formed pie-crust, Cool Whip, instant chocolate pudding and two "secret ingredients." Your main-stay, your staple, the one thing you have brought to every pot-luck since sophomore year in college because you've been so busy getting that 4.0, running a used car business and tending to your family, you haven't had time to memorize *Mastering the Art of French Cooking*. And someone just said in a sotto voice, clearly meant for you to hear, "I didn't know anyone still ate chocolate pie outside of Des Moines." You are outraged and a viperous look is not sufficient retaliation. Lie, my sweet. Lie.

"Funny you should mention Des Moines," you begin, with downcast eyes and a trembling voice, "That's where my favorite aunt was from. It's her favorite recipe. Well, my dear uncle's favorite recipe in fact. Oh, how he loved it." Now with happy memories of these two mythical people flooding your mind, look up, smile warmly, your eyes slightly misting over.

You then tell a story which combines this pie and some cherished element from the life of the person who was rude to you. Say she's into bulldogs. Then it's a story about how your relatives went on a picnic with a pie and their beloved bulldog and the bulldog ate the pie. If Ms. Nasty loves to canoe: out on a lake were your relatives when a big wave came along and tipped the pie right out of the boat. A few sentences should suffice, now, turn melancholy. "Of course, once she got arthritis, she couldn't cook anymore, so when I went to visit, I would make it for them. She would always say it was better than hers and he would always say it was excellent, but no one could make it as well as his dear Charlotte." Start crying.

"He died in his sleep one night, we all flew out immediately of course. I wanted her to come live with me. She was such a wonderful person. But she died herself the next night. Sleeping on the sofa. She couldn't face being without him." By now, at least three people in the room should be crying. Wipe away your tears; put on a brave face and say in the gentlest voice, "That's why I like to make this pie, to think of them, what kind and lovely people they were, how much they loved each other. I know it isn't fancy, but it brings back such warm memories." Everyone will now look at the person who was so offensive with unadulterated disgust. Problem solved.

The third person in your pantheon of heroines is of course Miss Piggy. Sigh. Raise your glass (champagne, naturellement) to that paragon of porcine perfection. And pay attention to the lessons she teaches through excellent example:

1. You could possibly fall in love with a person who is a different species and 1/3 your size. Let it happen. Revel in it. Ignore all common sense about mixing breeds (much less classes, religions, races, or ethnicities). Love is so precious, it must be honored. Love him (her) dearly, hold her (him) close.

2. Pet names are sweet, charming, and not for public consumption. Keep the "Kermieeeeee" for behind closed doors and sound-proofed walls.

3. Although all correct-thinking people are non-violent by creed, Miss Piggy instructs us that some people do not need sympathy or understanding, they need to be karate-chopped. Do your chopping with flair, finesse, and good sound effects.

4. Wear a tiara.

5. Occasionally over-act, it gets the blood going and if you can't stand a little attention, live in Nebraska.

- The Queen of England is the role-model you keep constantly before you in every public transaction. Never tell anyone this. But if it should happen to leak out allow me to assist you in dealing with those ignorant, twitching goats who bleat about how monarchies are repressive and how Her Royal Highness has robbed people, etc. ad nauseam. Read the sentence again. It doesn't say "Become a Queen, oppress people, live in a castle." The sentence says, "The Queen of England is the role-model you keep constantly before you in every public transaction." People who blather on about H.R.H.'s wealth are the same people who screech at the thought of paying inheritance tax or do not expect to receive any inheritance. Ignore the first group and repeat to the second group that you are not attempting to reinstate feudal landownership et al, you merely aspire to a public persona which does not resort to haggling, whining, bickering, cussing, shrieking and/or spitting to get through the daily round of errands, personal interactions and social celebrations.

- Don't talk about a subject you don't know anything about if there is a good chance you will get caught out.

- Vote.

- If one does not vote, Saints forbid, in every single election (high school, dog catcher, city manager, president,...) than you are not allowed to voice any sort of opinion at any time (until the next election, at which point you will immediately rectify your erring ways) on government (city, state, national), taxes, parking meters (controlled by city), who's in charge, condition of the schools, foreign policy (including police actions, wars, and armed peaces). You can now see the beauty of this. The time and energy you expend in voting allows you to vociferously complain (following, naturellement, the Diva's Code of Complaint—DCC). Now if you have some particularly irksome twit who complains vigorously to you about politics (not following the DCC), then you are entitled to ask, in the spirit of breathless inquiry, "So who did you vote for in the last elections?" If said twit begins a long harangue about s/he never votes, wouldn't vote, the system is corrupt... you shake your head sadly and remark in a voice full of remorse, "But if you didn't vote, you can't complain." If twit attempts to prolong the conversation, repeat the words, "We'll have to agree to disagree," until twit goes away.

- Give advice when asked, but only on the point in question. Never give advice that the person can't follow, has already disparaged and/or when the person has already decided what they are going to do. Read Carolyn Hax and Gretchen Rubin.

- Watch the Oscars.

- People who tell you something positive about themselves when they first meet you are lying. "Hi, I'm Janice. I really believe in open communication" means "I am a blow-hard, braggart, conversation-hogging troll." The woman who sent around a nasty e-mail my first day of work, then came hurrying over to my office to introduce herself "because I don't want your first impression of me to be from that e-mail, I really am a very nice person" had the nickname "she who eats her own children."

- People who instruct you that your relationship with them must be "fair" or "honest" when they first meet you are unredeemable, evil-hearted trolls who will stab you in the back.

- Be a feminist. You know those tiresome, mis-guided, kind of idiotic women who walk around saying that feminism is dead, or that they don't consider themselves to be feminists? Don't be like those kinds of women or I will have you kidnapped and put in an igloo with only *A Room of One's Own* and "The Yellow Wallpaper" until you come to your senses (or lose your mind).

- Every sentence you say in a fight must begin with "I," never "you." And never say the word "always." Note the difference between "I am so mad that you taped a baseball game over our wedding video" and "You always ruin everything."

- Never expect any one to give you money. Ever. If your best friend wins the lottery, you say "How wonderful for you!" not "When are you taking me to Ibiza?" When your dear, rich great uncle dies you say, "A wonderful man, how I shall miss him," not "I hope I get the Van Gogh."

Never expect presents for your birthday, holidays or weddings. NEVER EXPECT ANYONE TO BUY YOU ANYTHING, EVER. And don't ever buy a second gift for anyone who doesn't politely thank you for your first gift.

- With caveat of above edict in mind, say what you want: be it a kiss, a phone call, lower volume on the stereo, or the recipe of that orgasmic zucchini casserole.

- Pretend not to notice anything that can't be fixed immediately (either by you or someone else at hand) stains on coats, dust on the bookshelves, hideously wormy husbands.

- Call careful and gentle attention to anything amiss that can be fixed—spinach in teeth, spelling mistakes on documents, a girlfriend carrying on with the badminton team in the guest bedroom at this very moment.

- Simply because you have stated that you want something doesn't mean you will, in fact, receive it.

- Listen to the music that makes you happy—whatever it is. And don't sneer at other people's music taste. You are not getting into heaven because of your playlist and are you are not going to be denied heaven because of your playlist.

How to Behave like a Diva

We must reclaim the word 'Diva.' The true meaning, from the Latin, is goddess, related to the word divine. It means an exemplary woman, a rare and venerated woman, who moves through the world with loveliness and grace. It does not mean a troll howling for freebies, discounts, preferential treatment and she ordered off-white lilies and these lilies are ivory and she did not order ivory lilies and heads are going to roll and how can she possible cope with ivory lilies and on and on. No. That is not a diva, that is a child without a cherished auntie to have guided her properly. We all know that ladies who push themselves to the front are eaten by tigers. And we all know that men (the proper kind of man) can also be a diva. Divaness is hard work; it might not come naturally, but it is the highest possible attainment for any human: to bring wisdom, clarity and kindness to every situation. And here are the rules to follow to reach that apotheosis.

- Don't go to exasperation. Go to pity. It's not "Oh damn, you oaf, you slammed into me and dumped your coffee all down my new, sky-blue silk shirt. You ox. You bastard. You're going to pay for this." Yes, that's what the world needs, more rude twits. If the person didn't spill the coffee on you on purpose (and no diva would make a person so mad that she deserved to get coffee tossed on and then be anywhere in the vicinity when aggrieved person was armed with coffee), then you are the only rude one. And Divas are never rude without a really good reason. Divas say, "Good grief," or perhaps,

"Oh no." Maybe, "Ouch." Then they excuse themselves to clean up a bit. When they return, divas listen to the offender's sincere apologies and make dry-cleaning arrangements. But what if the coffee-splasher has vanished? Pity. Pity the poor, dumb, lost soul who has so injured his/her karma as to inadvertently hurt someone then deliberately refuse to make amends. The person is no better than a beast. Leave him or her to their assuredly miserable fate.

- Divas have studied and taken to heart Patrick Swaze's immortal words: "You are nice until it is time not to be nice." Thus, divas never insult anyone except on purpose. (See above). Or as the hoi polloi say, choose your battles.

- Divas don't wallow.

- Divas don't say "I'm so busy" or "I'm too busy."

- One can do a lot of good in the world if you aren't concerned about who gets the credit.

- Never be racist or sexist.

- Divas can be atheists or agnostics, but if they pray they pray "Lord, let me be worthy of being on Your side," not "Lord, be on my side."

- Divas are not prejudiced against any religion, although they are not under any compunction to be pleasant to individual proselytizers, acting, as ever, in proper moderation (i.e. slam the door or hang up the phone, yes; sic the dogs or scream profanities, no.)

- Divas know three languages:

1. English. Because this is written for people in the United States of America. People in other countries need so fewer lessons in personal management,

having social systems more interested in creating a social harmony and thus less celebratory of people all dashing off in different directions and proclaiming the right to do whatever they want whenever they want to. The French, Italian and Northern Scandinavian countries don't need it because they already have perfect style and the English don't need it since they are so firmly convinced they are superior, they won't listen to advice from mere Americans. Am I making sweeping over-generalizations? But of course, my dear. Divas have lots of judgments, not to mention opinions and a clear idea of how things ought to be.

2. Non-verbal communications. Your eye-brows speak volumes. Your hands sketch symphonic poems in the air. You have a glance that would shatter glass and one which would melt icebergs.

3. Another language.

• Divas are always interested. Always curious. Never nosy.

• In business situations, divas follow Field Marshall William Slim's timeless advice "You will neither eat, nor drink, nor smoke, nor sit down, nor lean against a tree until you have personally seen that your men [and women] have first had the chance to do these things. If you will do this for them, they will follow you to the ends of the earth."

• Divas always, always say 'thank you.'

• Divas know that being rich, beautiful and successful will not make you happy.

• Trolls honor Amundsen because he was first; divas honor Scott because he was good.

- Divas understand sometimes it is necessary to have mashed potatoes for four nights in a row for dinner so that they may go to their favorite café on a Saturday afternoon.

- Divas are at peace with their looks. Not that I said, "Your features are perfect." Or "You have had $5,000 worth of plastic surgery." Or "you should have $5,000 worth of plastic surgery." I said, "You are at peace." They have either accepted their looks as they are, they are in the middle of working with moisturizers or tweezers or gelatin capsules to improve trouble spots; or they have decided to attack such problem areas at some point in the future and, thus, are not worrying about them now. These are Diva's ONLY three choices: acceptance, action, or planned action. No whining.

- Divas are aware of "issues" both general and particular but they do not cause an unseemly fuss. A diva would rather pull every hair out of her head than tell a host/hostess the foods she dislikes or is morally opposed to but informing about allergies/asking about ingredients because of allergies is always allowed.

- A diva knows that sometimes one must give up on a relationship. Even if (especially if) she still loves the person, the person is related to her, she has known the person for years, and/or the person once saw her through a rough time.

- If you walk out of the house expecting to be insulted, you will be. Divas walk out of the house expecting everyone to be as kind and smart as their marvelous selves.

- A diva knows that happiness is not a zero sum game. An increase in someone else's happiness can never diminish a diva's own happiness. Casting cold water on someone else's happiness, big or small, will never increase her chances for happiness. Gloating in a discernible public way over another's problems will in no way lead to her happiness. Failing to celebrate another's joys will leave her alone on the days when she would most like someone to celebrate with and will insure that when things go wrong for her, others will take a particular and noted interest.

- Understand that the question "Do you like my haircut?" can only be answered after sufficient processing. If you are one of those tiresome people who say "I always tell the truth" on such matters, then you are clueless. Go away right this instant. Go out into the world and be truthful. More power to you. When you say something that stuns the dinner table and dissolves the hostess into tears, I hope there will be a diva on hand to smooth over the moment and comfort the poor dear; when you dare to say the truth at a moment when everyone else is ducking the issue, I hope a diva is on hand to applaud you. You might be (as long as you are not mean-spirited and quite equal in all your truth-dispensing) a good creature, but you aren't a diva. This essay has nothing for you. Away with you.

Divas believe they are "A participant in the doctrine of constructive ambiguity" (Vernon Walters). If they like the haircut, they say so immediately, loudly, repeatedly. If it is hideous process, process, process:

    d. What does the person think of it?

    e. Is there time and/or money to fix it?

If the person likes it—the diva likes it. If there is nothing to be done about it, then a diva likes it and finds something positive to say: "You have such lovely ears, this style shows them off so well!"

Please note—from one week before a wedding until 2 days after, every bride, every single one, is beautiful.

One petite exception: people who ask, "Do I look OK" often, relentlessly seeking approval, get a bland 'Yes,' nothing more. Exception to the exception: non-obnoxious teenagers get as much flattery as you can trowel on. Poor dears.

- Divas revere Winston Churchill. Divas adore Winston Churchill. When divas put on their pin-striped power suits and go to fight boardroom battles, they say softly to themselves "No one can guarantee success in war, but only deserve it" and "We shall go on to the end...we shall never surrender."

HOW TO BEHAVE
AT YOUR SPA

I KNOW FROM SPAS. I have been to many a spa and I have decided that I need to start a spa. The manager will be Bernice, a matronly, middle-aged woman. When you walk in, she shrieks at you "Get out! You don't need a spa! You look fabulous! How could we possibly help you? You look great!"

When you have to fill out the form and write down your age, she says that you could not be that old and insists on seeing your driver's license, at which point she cusses out the DMV for taking such an unattractive photo which does not do justice to lovely you. Then she plops you on the sofa, gives you whatever you want to drink (coffee, diet coke, daiquiri, shot of tequila….) and goes over what treatment you want.

The spa menu is printed (with prices) on a regular sheet of paper—only the treatments available that day are listed. You can call to make an appointment, but they have enough people working so that you can always just walk in to get a pick-me-up pedicure.

You want a facial? Well honestly, Bernice doesn't think you need one, but if you want one, ok. And if you try to get something drastic done to your hair, she asks you about your love life, your sister, your mom, and your work and if there is some problem, she will talk you out of a crew cut with blue highlights.

There are current issues of all trashy and up-scale design magazines on all the coffee tables and romantic comedies on flat screen TVs. There is a manicure/pedicure room for people who want to chat and a manicure/pedicure room for people who want perfect silence. No 'running water' music that makes you need to pee. The massage rooms have adjustable lights, temperature and music. If you want a body scrub while listening to Shania Twain, no problem. And none of this "couple's treatments"—if you are getting a massage, you don't want the significant other anywhere near. Boyfriend should be out hunting a mastodon for lunch, not fussing over his cuticles.

It is called 'Bernice's Beauty Spot.' It has valet parking (for free). When you leave you get a free milkshake—any flavor you want, including vodka. And yes, of course, they have soy milk, almond milk and cashew milk.

Bernice's Beauty Spot is located in a strip mall—on one side is a dry cleaner, a small shipping store and a take-away restaurant. On the other side is a medium sized-grocery store called Fred's.

When you walk into Fred's store, Fred is standing by the door. He greets you by name, then he takes whatever children you have away from you. Small children go to a sound proof play room staffed by certified nurses and PhDs in primary education. Older children are sat in front of TVs playing Smithsonian-produced movies about lemurs in Madagascar.

Then an apple-cheeked, freshly scrubbed 17 year old appears at your side, "How may I help you?" You can send this person on any errand you want—to pick up or drop-off dry-cleaning, mail letters, send packages, pick up take-away dinner. Or just send your assistant off to the milk aisle to get four gallons of skim. You can hand over your cell phone (or your assistant will have his/her own) to make calls—check if the car is ready to be picked up, get the time the movie starts, call your mother to say you are fine but in a very important meeting.

The store has full-spectrum lighting and NO background music. There are live plants (all for sale) placed at the end of each aisle and tall palm trees serve as a backdrop for the liquor section. There are plates of samples everywhere, guarded by cute college-age workers who flirt shamelessly with you.

After you have put everything you want in your cart, you hand your credit card and car keys to your assistant and walk to the small coffee shop at the front of the store, there are two sections—those who want to chat and one 'silent' section.

Your assistant stands in line, purchases your groceries and supervises their packing. All freezer items go in one insulated bag, fridge items in another bag, all extraneous packing is removed and sorted for recycling so that you do not have to take the aspirin out of the box, break the seal and take out the cotton when you get home. You don't have to deal with shrink-wrapped, tamper evident or child-proof anything.

Then your assistant will bring your groceries to your car, put them in the car (discreetly sweeping out stray crumbs and food wrappers), drive your car to the entrance—put in under the watchful eye of the doorman and come to tell you that you are ready to go.

This is how stores should operate—this is how life should be, but usually isn't. Going into a grocery store is a soul-draining task: florescent lighting, linoleum floors, bad music, and plastic as far as the eye can see. You fight your cart with one bad wheel, you stand in line for ages, you throw things into bags and trudge out to your car to dump everything in the back seat.

And spas can be just as bad—they are supposed to be

havens of peace, security and happiness—and what do you get? In Bali, BALI! the mother-ship of spa experiences! I had an excruciating day. The spa did not have (as advertised) lavender body scrub (yum), coffee body scrub (yum yum) or sangria body scrub (yum yum yum), they only had 'Javanese lulur' (ho-hum). The massage was useless. The 'flower bath' was a few wilted frangipanis, some bougainvillea (which has no scent) and a few twigs in tepid water. The "hair cure" stripped all the color out of my hair and made it so frizzy and dry, I didn't wash it for 4 days. And the music—plonk, plonk, plonk in irregular rhythms—aural Chinese water torture.

This is not what I and you—special, beautiful, wonderful you—this is not what we were born for; we were born for quiet, for beauty, for tender and kind people telling us gently how lovely and beautiful we are. Bernice knows this—she understands. She had a terrible first marriage, which she will tell you about and make you laugh. Then she will tell you how she learned to be true to herself and met a wonderful partner who brings her flowers on the spur-of-the-moment, takes her to Thailand for their anniversary, loves to give her foot massages, and has been known to go out in pouring rain to get ice-cream.

You go to Bernice's Beauty Spot for a hair-cut and come out with the name of a good divorce attorney and a healthy recipe for fish that your kids will actually eat. Go in for a facial so you will look good in the coffin, come out half-drunk and clutching a Will Smith movie DVD which will get you through until your next therapy appointment. Go in for a manicure so you look professional for your dissertation defense, come out with the joke which will make the whole committee laugh and forget you messed up your statistics.

Oh give me your tired, your wrinkles, your lost, your split ends, your chewed cuticles, your lonely, your chipped nail polish, your scared, your chin hairs, your under-appreciated, your scraggily bangs, your fear, your busy, your stressed, and your chaotic. Bernice and Fred will take care of you. Bernice and Fred are here for you.

HOW TO CHOOSE A CAFÉ

FRANKLY, DARLING, YOU'RE EMBARRASSING ME. Really dear, we need to work on this. I know your mother had so much on her mind she couldn't quite find the time to impart the necessary pearls of wisdom, and you weren't blessed with a sister who had a few good marriages and several great affairs who could take you in hand. But I don't want a repeat of last summer, with me having to turn the other way and hide under my *tres joile chapeau* every time you walked into a café. Yes, it's café time again and, darling, before you put one pedicured, Arche-clad foot (or, sigh, a lumbering, Birkenstocked foot) into a café. Do me, do the universe, a favor and memorize this.

First we need to define café. Starbucks is not a café. You may use the following wisdom in a Starbucks, as you are free to wear your best jewels to a McDonalds, but do not pretend your grandmama's pearls makes Micky D's a fine dining experience. Cafés are either old or they look old. They are singular, with a personality set by the owner, wait-staff and customers, not "corporate headquarters." They have espresso and sturdy chairs. They have wooden, marble, or zinc tables. They do not have menus in more than two languages (and if you are smart—you NEVER look at the menu anyway).

Now, how does one go to a café? First of all don't take this lightly, this is a vital element of being a member of human society, so consequential we must break it into steps for you. First, you have two choices. One is to be yourself. Go on in like a bull in Limoges shop. Be American. Be proud. Wear (I shudder) comfortable clothes: Gap clothes, baggy khaki shorts, tennis shoes, (I shudder) matching warm-up suits, sweat pants, sweat shirts, t-shirts with writing on them, comfortable walking shoes, anything from Magellan's, TravelSmith, Eddie Bauer, or Lands' End. Revel in your essential Americanness. Speak loudly. Order "water." Take out a calculator for figuring out the exchange rate, a pocket dictionary, maps, a (I shudder) camera, a cell phone, a computer (I feel sick). Maybe the waiter will be kind to you. Maybe he or she will see you as whimsical, as a busy person with many responsibilities.

But there is also the chance you will be over-charged, ignored, or given the wrong items. If this happens, you may not complain. Not a whimper of protest do I want to hear from your chap-sticked lips. You walk into a café where Proust sat, where Oscar Wilde sat, where Hemingway sat and you are dressed like a five-year-old on the way to play group, acting like a brat and you expect good service? *Sacre bleu*. It is utterly astounding to me that the good cafés of Paris haven't simply given all waiters license to dump scalding coffee on the heads of all people who walk in wearing sweat pants, bleating out instructions into cell phones and asking for ice.

Long ago, when I was a mere diva in training, I was visiting New York with my Papa. He asked, "Where do you want to go?" And I said, of course, "the Plaza." We went to the Plaza, but as we were about to get on a long plane ride, we were dressed like Americans about to go on a long plane ride, i.e. like kindergartners. So we were sat by the kitchen door. I saw more of the Plaza kitchen than the dining room. Lesson learned. You want to swing with the big cats, you better be in a cat-suit.

So that is your first lesson: if you act and dress like yourself then take the consequences. If you accept that going to a café is a heavy responsibility, shoulder your responsibilities and act like a grown-up.

Ah-ha, you want to act like a grown-up you say. Very well. I shall continue the lesson. How to go to a café. Second part: do your homework. Before I'm going to let you out of your hotel, you must learn the following words in the most commonly spoken language in the country:

Hello

Please

Thank you

I would like a coffee (or tea)

Notice I said, "your hotel," not "your hotel room." No, I don't want you sitting on the bed struggling over vocabulary with some horrid little phrase book. Go to the front desk--even if it's the owner's grandmother sitting on a sofa watching soap-operas--and start practicing. Fine, she might laugh. Fine, you are providing amusement for the world. There are worse ways to affect a person. Practice and practice until those four expressions roll off your tongue.

Second, find out (by examining posted menus at other, not-your-style cafés) the range of prices and common selections available. Get the cost of a cup of coffee down, doing the exchange rate in your head. Examine at least five menus, see what's usually available and the average price. Make sure you have twice that amount in the correct currency on you, some of it in small coins and bills.

Three, walk around a bit, see what part of town you like best and what cafés you like. Are you a plaza person? Student hang-out? Trendy? Fusty? See what the people are wearing in the kind of places you want to be.

Four: decide what (or who) to take with you. Now see, I told you to examine things thoroughly. It's not just the clothes, it's the accoutrements. In the States you can't go wrong with *Vogue* (British version only), *Town and Country*, or *Smithsonian*; *People* is acceptable only because it is so completely unacceptable, working with the 'it's so bad it's good' principle.

If you want to read *The New Yorker* or *The New York Times*, I suggest you ingest your coffee exclusively at Dunkin' Donuts. In Europe, any newspapers in the native language is allowed. Depending on the style of the café, a book is OK (and understand, love, by "book," I mean "a hardcover book," not some grimy paperback. Read paperbacks on airplanes between Seattle and LA). Or a plain-paper book in which you are writing is allowed (but if you act the teeniest bit pretentious, I'm going to instruct Edgar to dump a tray of lattes all over it. What? You don't know the difference between simply writing in a day-book and inscribing your most intimate deep thoughts in a personal journal with handmade paper and the I-Ching on the cover which your soul-mate gave you just before you left? I'm sorry, there's only so much wisdom I can impart at one time. I'll deal with pretentious writing later). Postcards are tricky, full details below.

Now if you are going for the full mufti effect, before you head out to your café, go to a store and get some food that requires a full kitchen to prepare. Artichokes are perfect. You can't cook them in a hotel, much less youth hostel. A few artichokes in a bag say, "I live in this city, I am not just passing through for two days trying to soak up enough culture to make up for growing up in a place where most recipes start 'open a can of cream of mushroom soup' and the men put on a suit to get married and to be buried."

Five: go back to the hotel room and get dressed. No, don't whine at me. If you are going to start in on how difficult this is, go get a coke at Micky D's and be done with it. You want to swim with the big fish, you got to put on a wet-suit. All of the first steps can be done while you are wearing whatever you want, but if you want to go to a café (and, honey, saying "to café" as if the noun is a verb is an offense deserving a no-holds-barred slap) you have to blend in. No, don't you start moaning about how you couldn't fit a little black dress and heels into the duffel bag you are schlepping around Europe for two months. You should have packed one good outfit with one good pair of shoes. No one cares what Cal Ripkin Jr. wore during warm-ups, but when it's game time, the man wore his uniform because he is a real man and not some plastic fly-by-night twerp. No one cares what a conductor wears during rehearsals, but when it's show-time, he or she is in tails. The things you need to see and learn in Europe are not all accessible while wearing jeans and a sweatshirt. Get dressed like a real person.

Six: choose the exact café you are going to bless with your presence. Yes, I understand that mere mortals just go to whatever café is around when they are tired and thirsty and hot, but then, if you are a mere mortal, this article is not for you. Go play with your Game Boy; get your refreshment from a soda machine. You aren't ready for a café.

Remember—never enter a café out of desperation. You may be a bit parched, but not in wilting stage. You are in control; you are the captain of your destiny. You do not make moves out of recklessness. You look around carefully. You sniff the air. You get your fingers ready, as if you are about to play a particularly tricky sonata. You listen closely. And then, after much careful deliberation, you pounce.

Now, you may look marvelous (of course you look marvelous) but if you mess up your entrance, you will show yourself as a mere amateur (and embarrass me). This is where most Americans stumble, might as well just go ahead and stamp "I have no sense of culture, grace, or appreciation of the finer things in life" on your forehead if you just collapse into the first empty table you come to. Darling, you must choose your table with as much concentration as you chose your bed linens, aperitif or best girlfriend. Of course, you should have scouted out the general floor plan during your reconnaissance mission, but some in-door cafés are hard to figure out until you are through the door and committed.

Don't panic, don't bolt. Stand. Look around. Where is the best location for people watching? Where is the good lighting? Which pictures on the wall best complement your complexion? Give yourself some time. No sudden moves. Maneuver, with deliberation, towards the prefect table. Yes, people are staring at you, but once you are settled, you will stare at all the newcomers too. You are part of the game. Don't wimp out. It doesn't matter if you have to saunter past ten empty tables, or ask people to allow you to pass, you are General Patton. You are on a mission for the perfect café table. Do not back down. Do not surrender. Do not accept compromises.

Once you are a bit more advanced, you can make your decision with a swift motion, glancing over the sunglasses in summer or while taking off your fabulous scarf and artlessly fluffing your lovely hair in winter, but in the beginning, you might need to just stand for a good fifteen seconds or so until you make your decision. We all need to crawl before we can run, nothing to be ashamed of.

So now you have a table, preferably in the corner (but not too far in the corner) or against a wall, or right up front by the sidewalk, anywhere where you have a commanding view of the proceedings. Now, don't ruin your momentum. Don't dump your bags on the table, bags go on the floor or on the empty chair. Purse and glasses on the table. No plopping into the chair: descend (watching *Gigi* a few times will help). Now fuss a bit, get out your accessories. Lay your pen by your book. Lean back in your chair. Get comfortable. Examine the neighboring tables in a circumspect manner. If you realize your neighbors are some sort of ghastly mutants (talking about any medical procedure, golf, the stock market, or computer programs), then you have my permission to get up and move, quietly, quickly and with a frightened glance back towards the miscreants, so that everyone in the café will know they are not real humans.

Ahh, now. Aren't you comfortable? Don't you feel at ease? You are part of the crowd, and yet, still your own unique and special person. And you are a little thirsty. Well that's the test, isn't it? If you have accomplished all these steps well, the waiter will come to you in a reasonable time. Now reasonable might be as long as five minutes. And he or she may go to some other customer first. No fretting, no fidgeting. If you have followed my instructions to the letter, you are completely in harmony with the universe in general and your café in particular and you are not being ignored because of who you are, but because the waiter is busy or it's the rule that all customers get ignored for ten minutes. (I told you, never walk into a café really tired or thirsty!).

Ah, now the waiter has come up to you. Follow closely. 1) Smile, not a stupid, attempting-to-ingratiate yourself smile. A grown-up, warm, mature smile. A smile that says, "Hello, I'm harmless. I can't speak your language, I don't fit into your culture, but I will try to be respectful. I will try not to embarrass you or me. Let's be mature about this." 2) say "Hello, a coffee please" in the language of the land. If the native language is English or some variation of English, say it in plain American English. Do not attempt to mimic accents or I will disinherit you. The response should be a slight nod of the head or waiter repeating the order back to you. If he or she pretends not to understand, say your order again in the same tone of voice and at the same speed. Not louder and/or slower. If he or she still pretends not to understand, then my dear you have chosen an evil café, and your waiter is the mis-begotten spawn of a dog and a weasel. Leave immediately. Resolutely ignore any further comments from any employee. Even if the owner himself prostates himself at your feet, walk over him and be on your way. Willful meanness should never be tolerated. I understand you don't have a great accent or the perfect clothes, but you tried your best and that is not to be mocked. Head out and start over.

Now, assuming the wait staff has behaved, you are in the lap of luxury. Rarely in life are things so good. You are in a good café, you are part of a good café. You are in the warmest, most lovely and cosseted place on earth outside your lover's arms. Revel in this. Relax. Commence your activities. People-watch. Eavesdrop. Read if you want. Oh no, that isn't a Fodor's is it? Good grief, what on earth were you thinking? Have I been speaking to a wall? All right, all right, apology accepted. We all make mistakes. Maybe I should have gone into more detail on books.

Anything by any major European author is fine, as long as it is impossible to tell what book it is. Any brownie points you might accumulate by reading Dostoevsky are immediately forfeit if it's possible to tell that the book is by Dostoevsky. No personal memoirs by anyone in this century except Churchill or D.V., following the above rule, of course. Plays or poetry are fine as long as you don't mutter so much as one trimeter aloud. Small press books are a guaranteed win. No self-help books. Ever. Going to a café is self-help. Reading a self-help book while in a café is like wearing a nicotine patch and smoking. No guide books. You read guide books on the plane over, in your hotel room, at the breakfast table, or at important sites. It's rather charming to see people sitting on the Spanish Steps or outside the Louvre reading guide books. If you read a guide book in a café you might as well wear a sign that says, "Every particle of information I know about sex came from three *Playboy* magazines I swiped from my older brother. I have no world experience whatsoever and it looks very doubtful I ever will."

As for postcards, pay close attention. Writing postcards is within the limits of acceptable behavior but you must walk the fine line between being obsequious and being ostentatious. Don't attempt to hide them, no sliding them under your newspaper when the waiter comes, but no spreading them out all over the table and muttering "do I send the Eiffel Tower to Aunt Mabel or Aunt Estelle?" And, yes, you can also address them at a café, but discretion my dear is so, so, so key. Don't haul out some ratty, old address book and flip through pages, little bits of paper fluttering away. Write ALL the cards you intend too, then stack them in alphabetical order and address them one at a time. Then put them all away. Child, I see you lick stamps in public and I will disown you.

At some point the waiter will come with your drink, you will be too busy engrossed in whatever you are doing to notice how long it has taken the drink to arrive. You will not, I swear by God in heaven, you will not stare at the waiter in the intervening time. Nor will you look at your watch or make pointed comments. You are in a café, you have placed your order, the order will arrive when the order arrives.

And when it arrives, give the waiter your grown-up smile and say, "Thank you," then immediately commence writing, or people-watching, or whatever you were doing. And now you've got a good two hours to enjoy yourself. If you need to use the facilities, make sure you plan it so that there is still at least 1/3 of your drink left and leave your pen, book, newspaper, whatever out on the table. Leave your wrap or hat but take your purse.

Ah, you have enjoyed yourself as much as humanly possible. You are ready to rejoin the hustle and bustle. Perhaps, if it's an inferior sort of café, the waiter will have brought you a bill. But probably you have been completely ignored since the drink was delivered (yes, dear, you can always order another, or a little something to nosh on, but remember, you should know what the basic choices and price ranges are—so don't ask to see the menu, just ask for what you want. If you need to revert to English, that's all right, as long as you continue to say 'please' and 'thank you' in the local language).

So now AT LEAST twenty minutes before you need to, or feel like you would want to be gone, ask for the bill. Either catch the waiter's eye and make that little motion as if you are signing your name or, if he or she comes close enough to you, simply say, "May I have the bill, please." Don't worry if you don't get a reaction or don't get the bill for ten minutes. These things take time. The bill may come as a little piece of paper, or it may be a number thrown at you. Don't be afraid to ask for the sum to be written down. Now, pay the amount. Do not choke at the price, don't argue unless it is enough to buy as small car. Pay, and if it is not an unreasonable price, leave a small tip, not too much, not too little.

If you have asked for the bill twice and have waited twenty minutes, leave a small pile of money, equal to what the average price you noted at other comparable cafés cost, gather your things and leave. If accosted by the waiter, point at the table and say, "My train is leaving." And leave.

Be sure to note the name and location of the café, if it was bad, you can be sure to ignore it. If it was good, you can use the name as currency, pay back a friend's kindness or secure future kindnesses by saying, "Oh, you are going to Manchester, I went to the nicest café there, etc." The name of a good café is more valuable than the name of a good restaurant.

Now for the special situations. First one: going to a café with a friend and/or a cell phone. One, people in front of you always have absolute precedence over someone on the other end of a phone. Always, darling, no exceptions. Phone calls when you have a person sitting with you are kept at 30 seconds. No, I'm not going to give you any special dispensations. Thirty seconds or I will take that toy away from you.

Here's the second rule of going with friends: if you are discussing anything boring, you must whisper. No options. "Yes, Mummykins loves you very much and I'll be home in an hour" is intended for the ears of one person and only one person. Don't inflict it on anyone else. This law includes all talk about work, weekend plans, anyone's health, as well as all 12-step, yoga, church, mediation, finger-painting or tofu-cooking class. Please note ANY and all discussions about postcards, who has written to whom and what was written, are by definition, boring.

Now, if, on the other hand, you are talking about something rather smashing, then you are allowed, nay, encouraged, to talk in a normal or slightly raised, tone of voice. But no cussing or smutty talk, there's no need for it, child.

"So I walked in, cleaver in hand, and there they were, on the bed, going at it like bunnies, heaps of clothes strewn around the floor. Oh, I was beyond livid. I just walked over and grabbed them and started hacking. No mercy. Bits flying everywhere. And when I came to my sense, there they were, little pieces of couture Armani and Dior fluttering everywhere and those two huddled under the covers. But I was not satisfied, not a bit. I lusted for more. So I raised my cleaver again and advanced. Chopping and slashing, quite out of control. And then again a brief rest, to survey the damage. Every suit he owned was turned into a heap of dust rags. I dropped the cleaver on the mess, walked to the dresser where she had laid her signature long string of pearls, which, as we all found out, weren't individually knotted. Pearls everywhere. And before I left, I took her purse from the hall table and left a message for her husband, pretending I was from Jewels, you know, that fancy strip-joint. Said I would send it to the address on the driver's license. Which, of course, I did, third class naturally. Just like them." You can have this conversation in a café in the world at any volume. No problem. And I think you would WANT to have this conversation in a café.

Here is another excellent conversation to have in a café: you're ending your love affair with the ambassador because his wife is coming back from her vacation (*avec her petit ami*) in the Seychelles and you've decided to become a nun. You want to do this in an apartment? After he leaves, you're left alone and what are you to do? Call a friend. No, no, no. Go to a café, bring up the fact that you're leaving, let him plead. Let the other customers takes sides. Get several opinions, sort it all out. Then if you storm out, he will have people around to console and counsel him; if he leaves, you have a built-in support group. (Although the words "support-group" should seldom leave your mouth. Decent people don't over use that expression).

And of course, if you go to a café, you must understand that there might be some dramatic scene and you are obliged to jump right into the middle of it, especially if you end up in a front row seat. No hiding behind your sunglasses. Get in there and give your opinion. Participatory democracy is sometimes a heavy burden but you mustn't duck your obligations.

Second tricky issue: going to a café with a computer. Don't. Just don't. You may, under very special circumstances as a regular customer, bring one in. You may also use one if you are a college student in a college town and you can't bear your dorm room for one more moment. But otherwise, just stick to coffee shops in airports, or, better yet, stay home. If you must, simply must, lug in your little laptop and set it up and pretend that you are oh-so cool, hard-working hip-cat and not the ridiculous dweeb you are, then sit in the back, way back, in the worst seat. And no complaining about the time it takes to get a drink or the bill. And if someone dumps their Orangina on it, don't come crying to me.

Third tricky situation: how to be a regular customer. This takes time and finesse. And, as usual, there are many steps which you must work through, no rushing it. First, when you move to a new town (or if you have finally decided to join café society) you must scout out ALL the options. Nothing is worse than spending six months developing yourself at a café and then discovering a more perfect one a mere two blocks away. Tramp those streets my dear, look into every one in the neighborhood where you work/live. Ideally you should discover two or three that work for you. For example, I now have one to read books and/or write letters in, one for Saturdays or Sundays, and one to get a coffee to go in; I also know a good café in two other neighborhoods that I can go to when I'm in the area. But this took about four weeks and lots of bad coffees, icky waiters, and patience.

Once you have figured out which one you want to grace with your regular presence, remember the basics: Never over-tip. Don't try too hard. Go at least once a week. If they have one of those 'coffee-plans,' get the card and do get it stamped every time you go. If it's counter service it will take longer to get known, but if it's table service, you should around the fourth or fifth trip, begin to drop small bits of information about yourself to the waiter. Waiters love to gossip about customers. But don't expect too much too soon. You can't say 'the usual' until waiter does, and the first few times the waiter asks, "the usual"? you have to say 'yes' even if you don't feel like it. But if the waiter makes no sign that this is the 12th time you've been in four weeks, cut your losses and go.

After a few months, you should have a nice equilibrium, even if it's nothing definite—they shouldn't be pulling chairs out for you, but you should get a nod of recognition, it should be easy to get his eye—and you are allowed to make some mistakes, to misjudge your time and say "Oh, didn't notice it was five already, I need to go, may I have the bill please" and it should appear immediately.

And now you can expect your favorite imbibement, coffee with a drop—a drop I tell you—of almond essence; decaf with Madagascar (or, in a pinch, Seychelles) vanilla; cappuccino with chocolate milk. I had a café in Cyprus with a fabulous/hideous hangover cure (pureed lettuce and carrots and something green I don't even want to think about).

You can even take friends—but be very careful. I once had a lovely beauty salon which I introduced to a friend. Alas, we did not remain friends, and several months later I walked in, ready to escape the world, to discover this woman who I now dislike sitting next to me for 45 minutes while we both had pedicures.

Eh bien, this is all you need to know; now memorize every word. Think of it as your dowry.

How to be an Optimistic Pessimist:
My Banana Tree has Bananas and I am Going to Go Watch a Snake Movie

I never realized how much of a pessimist I am until I found bananas on my banana tree. (And please don't start the whole pedantic thing about how actually it's a banana 'plant' not a 'tree'—this is not a botany text. If I say it is a banana tree, it's a banana tree.) My banana tree (don't argue with me) had bananas. A miracle. A totally unexpected miracle.

Yeah, I got the tree (i.e. Luxchman, my gardener, found it for me), I planted it (i.e. I asked Luxchman to plant it), I watered it (i.e. Luxchman watered it) and I watched it—but I never expected it to actually, you know, grow and make bananas. But it did.

And then, this totally blew me away, the rose bushes made roses: actual roses, rose-colored roses, rose-scented roses. My fig tree produced figs. My lime tree made limes. My almond tree bloomed. Guavas on the guava tree—papayas on the papaya trees. I guess it would be really a miracle if the guavas showed up on the papaya tree, but for me, quietly hard-core pessimistic, I never thought any of the plants I bought, paid to be put in the ground, watered and watched would actually DO anything. My, unexamined, underlying assumption was that they would turn yellow, sickly, droop, lose leaves, and give up the ghost.

My deep-seated pessimism is the reason I don't watch

romantic comedy movies. One friend, in that way of using the wrong word that is actually right, calls me 'fluffy.' I would seem to be a pink frilly skirt, rhinestone barrettes, kitten heels, fuchsia purse, card-carrying 'chick-lit' fiend. No such luck. I like happy endings, but I don't believe in them enough to watch the movies or read the books. Those rugged men who are too-good-to-be-true are too-good-to-be-true. Which is why I like shark movies.

You know the movies that start with the helicopter moving over a vast stretch of water towards a deep sea research platform which has recently had an unexplainable glitch in the super computer? I snuggle into my comfy chair, popcorn at the ready. I love, love, love, those opening scenes in which the expert explains to the new-comer about the triple-secure, backed-up safety doors, which will fail in about twenty minutes. Pessimism rules!

I love snake movies—the little ship bravely chugging down the Amazon looking for medicinal plants and finding huge predatory anacondas. The inexplicably large crocodile footprints by the side of the quiet lake. The flock of bats which are starting to act oddly. The deserted space ship which is broadcasting an unusual signal. The underwater rock formation with the peculiar cellular structure. Love them.

But not truly scary movies, not horror flicks. I like movies with fake violence and nothing that could, by any stretch of the imagination, happen to me. Woman attacked in a subway station, no, no, no. Woman attacked on interplanetary space ship—no problem, as I am never going to set foot on an interplanetary space ship. I am not going to set foot on any kind of submarine, I am not going to research tropical diseases in tropical jungles, I am not going down volcano craters, or up the Andes. I am not interested in experiencing uncharted anything; dealing with my grocery store reorganizing the shelves is difficult enough.

The Transporter (first one)—excellent. I am not going to hire anyone to move illegal goods. *Rouen*, actually anything with Jean Reno, great! I am not going to hire professional hit men. Anything with Vin Diesel! *Matrix* was ok, but trying too hard to be intellectual. *Minority Report*, *Pirates of the Caribbean* (first one), *Terminator* 1, 2 and 3, very good, especially as *Terminator* 3 has a car chase between a pick up and a truck-crane, that is a nice touch. I always appreciate it when someone thinks about the car chase.

And Jet Li, Jackie Chan's dark twin, now there's a guy who makes good movies. Nothing like watching some good old punching! What could be more relaxing? The movies are like Bollywood films (or 'filmi' as they say) in that you get drawn into a universe that looks like yours, but isn't.

It is safe to watch the movie because it portrays a universe you will never visit. For example, Hong Kong films have a weird obsession with wound protection. I still don't know what the underlying cultural force at work there is, but in HK films the hero will spend 15 minutes decimating hordes of bad guys, then show up in the next scene with a band-aid on his forehead. He's been shot, impaled, whipped, and mangled. He's got broken ribs, a cut hand, bruised every-thing and limps—but there's that little band-aid on his forehead. When there is a group of good guys there will be several band-aids in evidence in the obligatory 'meeting the day after the fight' scene. So, while you watch the fight, you can concentrate on where you think the band-aid will appear.

Furthermore, since there have been so many movies, fights have a whole classification system [like car chases in American movies—you have 'matched' vehicle chases

(James Bond film with two race cars on ice), 'unmatched' vehicle chases (the Hummer vs. VW Bug), lots of cars after one car (*Blues Brothers*), etc...]. So, you have hero against multitudes, hero and gang against villain gang and on to the good subsets: hero with handicap (Jackie Chan fighting with hands handcuffed to disconnected steering wheel), fight in enclosed space, fight while trying to stop object from touching the ground (usually priceless vase or bomb), and, my favorite, fight when hero is carrying unconscious person, who is swung around like a battering ram.

And you get these plot points coming from nowhere. Like hero asks sidekick, "Did you used to work under Lt. Chan?" Sidekick says, "Yes, he was a nice guy." Hero shoots sidekick and says, "Chan was a bastard." Hero and sidekick have been buddies about two weeks in movie time—and sidekick has never been shown to know, much less assist, bad guys. Why did that happen?

Or the scene in which hero takes innocent-female-caught-in-cross-fire home, goes into kitchen and goes whackita whackita whackita with knives to make dinner. Which looks good but tastes awful. She goes into kitchen and goes whackita whackita whackita with knives and you think, "Oh I know what happens next: she is great cook, so he falls for her." Then you see evil black smoke coming from the wok. She looks sad, then you hear hero's voice say, "It's ok." Female turns around and there is hero with tray, nicely arranged with carry-out boxes. He went out and bought dinner! My pessimistic heart melts. This never happens in American movies. American men don't even understand the concept that a woman could be lousy cook and a quick exit to corner sushi stand, much less arranging objects on a tray, is what is called for.

American movies are more like *Forrest Gump*—am I the

only American who loathes this movie? —way too happy.

Casablanca and *Lovely Actually* work because the people you like get their hearts smeared all over the pavement. Just like real life. Humphrey and Emma Thompson are devastated. Hugh Grant is in love with a ditz. One guy is in love with his best friend's girl. A man marries a woman he can't communicate with, so their joy is prolonged until they are mutually fluent in each other's language, then they will get divorced. At which point the man will go on a tropical vacation to forget his pain and, ignoring the advice of the local waitress who warns him that the sharks have been acting strangely, the man will join a tour group going out for a perfectly innocent day-sail with a little snorkeling at a beautiful reef. Cue ominous music; cue me on the sofa with a Diet Coke and a fruit salad made from my own fruit trees.

HOW TO BE A BAD
EXAMPLE AUNTIE

EVERY DECEMBER WHEN I WAS A CHILD MY MOTHER WOULD ANNOUNCE IN A SEPULCHER TONE OF VOICE THAT "THIS YEAR WILL BE A SMALL CHRISTMAS." This was said with deep regret and seriousness, as if the previous year the Rockettes had stopped by to serenade us before we jetted off to Capri with Aerosmith and the Rolling Stones. Hah.

Every Christmas was a "small Christmas" in my childhood, thus creating lasting psychological damage. We had a fireplace, but (brace yourself) no Christmas stockings. I mean, no filled stockings. They could have at least told us not to hang them up, but no. Up they went and down I came on Christmas morning to find my stocking hanging limp and forlorn. Except for the evil year my parents had an evil idea. I came down that year and saw my sticking was full, stuffed, bulging. Oh the joy in my little heart! Oh the happiness! Oh the sheer bliss, delight, glee and ecstasy—my dream came true! Until I walked closer and saw that it was full of puzzle pieces. They had bought a 1,000-piece puzzle and filled all three of our stockings with the pieces. Evil. And their excuse? It wasn't about the money. They just didn't like to shop. They didn't think children needed more than three or four Christmas presents. They were busy with community service projects.

Yes, by some unbelievable unpleasant trick of fate, me, Little Miss Let's Go Shopping, Little Miss Over-Decoration, Little Miss Could We All Dress Up and Eat Breakfast on Fine China got born into a family of Walk Gently on the Earth types. It was Let's Watch TV vs. Let's Go Bird-Watching my whole childhood—and guess who won.

My mother sneaks into other people's gardens and weeds for them. She volunteers for various organizations; she was the president of her church. She is never bitter, never sarcastic. My mother's idea of joy is 5 cubic yards of mulch, a shovel, and a free afternoon. My father's idea of joy is hiking boots, a free day and a long, uphill path with scenic views and hungry grizzly bears. If anyone in my family is hungry, they grab a piece of fruit. They never know any of the top ten songs or hit movies. They like classical music. They don't watch TV. They are alien life forms. So you see why I need to sit quietly and eat lots of chocolates to keep the balance of the universe—it's a duty and a sacred responsibility.

People who meet my family say, "Oh! They are so nice." Well, yes, they are very nice. They are nicer than me; they are sweet, funny, kind, and helpful. That's not the point— the point is how did I get related to them? Do you have any idea how difficult it is to be around people who don't nurse grudges, don't resort to irony, who are honest and kind to strangers? Utterly exhausting.

The point is what do you want from dinner? If you want well-balanced nutrition, vitamins, minerals, talk to them. Talk to them if you want a serious discussion about school curriculum, How to Help Your Community, How to Sweat (biking around Tasmania, biking around Hawaiian Islands, biking across the USA...) and How to Get Rescued by Park Service Personnel When You Bike in a Blizzard. Those are stories I could not tell you.

If, on the other hand, you want some totally useless facts (the Phantom of the Opera's name is Erik in the original story and he is an architect) and a funny story about driving four hours to see, in the middle of a desert, a hole with water in it, then I am your woman. When one of the nephews came to visit he found a pack of cigarettes in my car. "You smoke?" he asked, horrified. The truth is I don't, but there was something in his tone of voice. What could I do? "Yes," I said, "It relaxes me."

My nephews and nieces have grown up surrounded by good people who do not drink alcohol. They eat healthy, home-cooked, nutritious food. They share. They play sports and do good deeds. They are pleasant. But at some point in this life those latent genes which are floating around the family, collected in me but I am sure dispersed somewhere in their veins as well, may assert themselves. One of them may get snarky. One might feel jealous or unsettled; caustic and acerbic words might creep into someone's vocabulary. And I don't want him or her to feel surprised or worried. Cynicism is part of their birth-right. And if it ever manifests, here I am—bad example auntie, ready to ease the transition into *la vie sardonic*.

HOW TO
BEHAVE IN THE
MIDDLE EAST

It's DIFFICULT ENOUGH TO GET THROUGH daily life at home, but when you move overseas, everything becomes more confusing. All of the normal problems at work are compounded because you are dealing with many different cultures. The first essay goes over some general points about how to cope as an expat professional in the Middle East. The next two address something that is rarely discussed, when you live in the Middle East, you usually have hired help, which as a middle-class citizen of Canada, America, the United Kingdom or a European country, you are probably totally unprepared for. You have spent your whole life cleaning your own home, tending your own garden, washing your own car and suddenly you are crying because your gardener has hacked your oleander to pieces. This is not something that you can complain about to friends at home. But you can complain to me. I have been there—coming home to find my hand-made rug has been cleaned with steel wool. It's difficult to balance the fact that you now have people you need to take care of with the fact that they are constantly doing things you don't want them to do. After setting a vacuum cleaner on fire and breaking the washing machine, the woman who cleans my house came to me in tears because her son's school fees were due and she didn't have enough money. All the philosophy courses in the world can't prepare you for that moment—do you fire her, refuse to cover the fees or pay? It's not a theoretical 'what to do about poverty' but a person standing in front of you and you know that if you don't come up with the money, that child will not graduate high school, ruining their chance for a good job. Darling, I gave her the cash. The last essay gives a glimpse of daily life in a small town.

HOW TO BEHAVE WHILE LIVING IN THE MIDDLE EAST

- Never deliver bad news.

  Do not complain about this because you will compound your error—you will be viewed as both dense and tactless. First, learn to communicate in terms of realistic needs, not questions—"I must have the report on Thursday"—not "Will the report be ready on Thursday?" Second, if you have to ask questions, make them specific: not "Do you like my new sweetie?" but "I think I am falling in love with her, do you think there is a chance we will have a long and happy relationship?" Third, as you will never hear "no"—pay attention to the answer. "Maybe" means "no way in hell;" "yes" means "very small chance."

- You can't worm the bad news out of them, even if you try.

  Middle Easterners can work eight hours a day for ten years sitting next to someone and never know if the person is married, much less has children—they are the undisputed masters of not saying what they do not want to say.

  Think of it this way: Ramadan lasts a MONTH, then there is a 3 day Eid, and 40 days later, another 3 day Eid—about 34 days with non-stop relatives! Imagine their self-restraint, their ability to put up with those they don't want to talk to or see! And imagine their reaction to your self-actualized whining about how your mother missed your kindergarten graduation and your father wasn't supportive of your acting career.

They will tell you what they want to tell you, when they want to tell you and how they want to tell you—and what they tell you will have a very good chance of not being exactly the truth in North America/European terms. It never fails to amaze me that expats will go to another culture to "learn"—they will eat the food, wear the local dress but steadfastly maintain that their way of communicating is the best and other people better get in shape.

[If you want to know something in the Middle East, shut up. Listen, watch, who is talking to who and when and why—if the university says that there will not be a vacation next week but your officemate asks if you can please water the plants as he will flying home for a week—book your tickets to Thailand.]

- Cause and effect are not connected.

This is a big issue—often the first major stumbling block to expats. Expats think that if you do something bad you should be punished and if you do something good, you should be rewarded. Ha ha ha.

In the Middle East, sometimes that happens, but if you do something wrong in the Middle East the first order of business is to find someone else to blame it on, then deny all responsibility (see above point about never deliver bad news). Hence bad things 'happen'—passive tense, author/actor unknown.

Events are at the discretion of the will of God, so if you get sick, it was not because you were up all night smoking shisha. You simply did not have the luck. This will annoy you to no end, then you will mess something up badly and, as you sit at your desk awaiting the axe, here comes your boss with a promotion.

• Nothing is planned or addressed until the last minute.

You go to the post office to mail a letter. You stand in this line, the envelope is inspected, you are told to go to THAT line, you go there and the envelope is inspected, you then go to third line to buy the stamps. You are just in the act of placing the stamps on the parcel when you are told that the envelope you are trying to send is "not good"—you must go to a store and buy a new envelope.

You are told to go to police station to get your national ID card, you arrive, fill out paperwork, wait an hour, then you will be told that you need to pay the equivalent of $50 in one dollar bills. *Why didn't someone tell me this?* you shriek, thinking you could have brought the money with you or run out and got it while you were waiting. Shrug.

Now, of course, you don't have time to get the money before the police station closes, which means you come back tomorrow—spend another hour waiting, hand over the money, at which point they ask you for 4 pictures of yourself. You have a little breakdown.

[First—if you are doing anything involving a government office, carry a lot of money in small bills, 10 passport pictures of yourself and every official document you have (including marriage certificate and high school diploma). Second—if you are embarking on a bureaucratic journey, do not ask how long it will take, ask what they steps are. Ask "What do I do first, and then, and then..." Third—give up all hope.]

Oh my dear people, this will drive you to distraction—but what is not clear until you have lived in the Middle East for a while is that since the whole culture is set like this, it works perfectly for everyone. There is simply so much going on, so much to process that you can't possibility keep up. All too soon you will find yourself buying birthday presents ten minutes before the party, not to mention throwing a dinner party and forgetting to invite your guests until 20 minutes before the food is ready.

- You need to be pleasant all the time about everything.

A few expats can get away with being rude in the Middle East but they are rich, hated and constantly drinking tea that someone has spit in. Be nice. Channel your inner happy space. Spend a year in Montana before you move over. I am not kidding. Pleasant and friendly in the face of anything will get you where you want to go—people will literally laugh at you if you lose your temper. I am not saying it is easy—I am saying it is necessary.

This is a subtle but important point, something that becomes clearer the longer you are in the Middle East. It is the people with the least power who can poison your life. The "tea assistants" who bring you a tiny cup of tepid tea make $25 a month, sleep 10 to a room, and haven't seen their country in two years. You have every advantage and oops! Did you just yell at one of them because they forgot to put sugar in your tea? Oops! There goes your tax return which you gave them to mail, into the trash. Accident. The photocopies you were looking for? Floating in the wind. Ask one of them for pens, paper, scissors, glue, paperclips—shrug.

Be nice, be nice, even through gritted teeth, be nice.

- It is impossible to be pleasant all the time about everything because things can go spinning out of control very quickly and very irreversibly.

You dash into a department store to buy some batteries and the clerk runs your credit card through. The machine doesn't work—three other clerks come over, the manager strolls by, various other customers give their opinion. It is over an hour before you can leave. All the groceries in your car have melted into oblivion, except the melted chocolate ice cream stain which remains forever on your car seat. You tried to get away but all the other actors grabbed your arm and told you that you must stay.

You go to buy a satellite card, go back and it's another guy, go six more times, not ready yet, finally you get it and it works, but five channels are missing—and although they were included in your contract, oops, now you have to pay extra, on and on it goes—making the Ring Cycle look short and devoid of plot or conflict in comparison.

• You can never know what will unlock the puzzle or restore the order.

You can go to the bank four times to get your ATM card—fruitless, wasted hours spent and then suddenly the fifth time you go, there is the woman with the password, the computer is working, the clouds part: you are standing in the sunshine with a working ATM card. Quick—go sacrifice a sheep.

• As you can never know what will go haywire or what will restore order, you need to get way out ahead of everything and never leave anything to fate.

Constant vigilance combined with unstinting supervision. This is your new motto. You think you can let one aspect of your life simply glide. Ha ha ha. This is what makes your life so constantly tiring, you can't predict anything, you can never ever say: *today I will do this*. Never ever. The lights will fall down, the sink will start to leak, the tailor will make your dress two sizes too small, ants will take over your kitchen counter, your cell phone won't turn on, you will break into hives, the store will be in the middle of being repainted so no one will be able to locate anything, jumping spiders will invade your wardrobe and you won't be able to find contact solution in any store within 100 miles. And that's just the first hour of your day.

- It's not about the money.

Expats are used to being able to threaten over money: "If you don't do it I won't pay you." Ha ha ha. Middle Easterners are perfectly willing to do something that will cause them great financial hardship if it will keep their honor or piss you off if they don't like you.

Newbies whine, "They are cutting off their nose to spite their face," people who have lived in the Middle East for a while say, "Money is not the most important thing—respect is. Take it slow, build a relationship…"

Expats want to keep the contact at a certain level—I pay, you do X. The better way is to go local—think about a rug merchant. He has a rug. He paid a certain price for it, but what he sells it for is up to him. Maybe he will sell it for less than he bought it if he thinks it will open up a long relationship with a customer. Or he will charge five times the original purchase price if he thinks he can get it.

There is no "price," no "actual price," no "what the market will bear," no "best deal." There is only one figure that matters—what it is worth to you. I know, this conceptual framework gives expats the heebie-jeebies, but what can you do? Nothing. The price is what you are willing to pay—do you want it or not?

- Forget about lawyers.

Nothing could be less effective than "I'll sue you."

- Forget about discussing "women and the veil."

You will never understand so leave the topic alone.

- You have to keep in constant contact with all the people with whom you have any sort of relationship.

If you buy a computer you have to stop by the computer store every few weeks without fail because if you don't, when you have a problem, they won't help you. If you buy a car, go see the dealer every few weeks to say hello, build up a reserve of good will. Chat with all the secretaries. Smile at the shopkeepers you pass on your way to work. Wave at your gardener, compound watchman and the guy who sweeps the leaves. Send goodwill SMS messages at the beginning of Ramadan and for the two major *Eids*.

Think of Jane Austin—trying to write her novels with people constantly interrupting her, that's your life now. You have to take it at the tide. Accept those last-minute invitations. Leave the shopping in the bags on the kitchen counter and go have tea with your neighbor when she calls.

- You will know excruciating details about everyone else.

There are few big stores, and anyway, big stores aren't much fun. So you start to collect a whole passel of small shops for specific items. Fruit stand, shawarma stand, car repair, the guy who brings you bottles of water, taxi driver, gardener, print shop, dry cleaner, tailor, corner store for milk and yoghurt, bakery, house cleaner, carpenter, butcher, stationary store, jeweler, pharmacy, perfume store... And all these people are related in a vast, unfathomable web of family, work, and living-near-each-other connections. And most of these people see expats as their personal, long-running soap opera.

You run into the guy who works at your dry cleaner in the grocery store, his friend works at a car-repair shop where one of your friends was today, so you hear (is it second- or third-hand?) about your friend's carburetor. The guy who comes to paint your front door tells you that your boss's sister just had a baby.

• Everyone knows everything about you.

Your maid will tell everyone about your new sofa. Your neighbor's maid will tell everyone whose car was parked all night in your driveway. You get into a taxi and, not thinking, say 'home please' and although you have never seen him before in your life, he drives to your house. Don't let it get to you because (see next point)

• There is stuff you will never know about anyone.

You will work with someone for five years and at their going-away party you will find out they are the world's leading expert on Eastern European church architecture. You will have heard (from the woman who gives you manicures at the beauty salon) all about his wife, and his girlfriend, the new wife and the new girlfriend. You will have heard (from the guy who came to fix your internet) about his all-red bathroom with a mirror on the ceiling. You will have heard (from the guy at the Turkish restaurant you go to sometimes) that he has twenty identical pairs of black lace-up shoes. But that he has 14 published books, a medal of honor from the

Pope, 2 fan clubs and a key to the city of Paris will not be revealed until you mention his name in passing at a party back home and everyone gasps, "You know him? Honestly? Can you get me his autograph?"

- As you will never know the truth about anything, you will have to judge people and situations with your gut.

  Whoever you are talking to knows more about you and the situation than you know about them or the situation. So you will need to improve your "face reading ability," something nature gives us to help figure out if we are looking at a friend or enemy, sometimes called "instinct," "second sight," or "lizard brain." Peer into the person's eyes and ask yourself, "Do they look nice?" Practice this. Work on your intuition.

- You represent your country every moment of the day.

  Unless you live in a big city, work in a large company, and live in an all-expat compound, you will meet people every day who have never met someone from your country. You are it. You have the ability, with a smile and pleasant behavior, to break down a lot of negative stereotypes. Be nice, be nice, be nice.

- As most people can't tell the difference between American, Canadian, Australian, and English accents, and we all have bad days, sometimes it's ok to lie about your country of origin.

  Canada has such a good reputation, pretending to be a Canadian after a particularly vile hissy-fit won't hurt them. The English are always sure they are right so behaving badly and blaming them is acceptable. Australians are pretty laid back so they can also take the blame.

HOW TO HAVE
HELPFUL HELP

Part 1: You are Not in Control

People who have never had a housecleaner, gardener, tailor, or a person who brings you tea at work believe that having said help is a hedonistic luxury. This is because they believe in the Vulcan Mind Meld. But the Vulcan Mind Meld does not exist, which you will figure out as soon as you have a housecleaner, gardener, tailor, or person who brings you tea at work.

Newbies to the Middle East learn of the ease of hiring domestic employees and become overjoyed. Old-hands sigh and place bets on who will freak-out first. Because it's impossible to explain to a newbie, try as we might, that housecleaners have their OWN IDEAS about what a 'clean' house means and explaining, pointing, demonstrating, getting frustrated, and finagling will have ZERO effect— they know what they want to do and they will do it.

I have a small pair of decorative birds. I hate decorative birds that appear to be kissing. My housecleaner loves decorative birds that appear to be kissing. So every time I come home, their beaks are touching. I move them. She moves them back. 4 years and counting.

If you say, "Oh that is ridiculous," you are a newbie. If you counter me with the story about how your housecleaner shakes out the 'welcome mat' and replaces it upside down or folds the towels the *wrong way* or over-waters the plants so they all die, or insists on using toilet bowl cleaner on the kitchen sink, then you can sit down next to me.

"Just explain patiently," recommends the newbie. Sweet little newbies, they are so soft and clueless, like baby pandas. I like to tape newbies who gush, so I can play their words back to them when they show up in my office frothing and screaming that the tea assistant brought over-sugared tea again and why can't he... Exactly. He can't, he won't, he doesn't want to, he is physically incapable of making tea with less than 8 spoons of tea. And what are you—with your Oxbridge first, Wharton MBA, and $400 shoes—going to do about it? Or more to the point, what can you do to a man whose yearly income is less than what you spend on sparkling water? Nothing. He has been screamed at by better than you and your attempts at bonhomie are useless. You aren't friends. You work, he works. You think your work is more important because you make a lot of money but if you look at it in terms of impact—your salary pays for what? If the two of you were sat down and asked, "Who are you helping? How is your work benefiting people?" who would have a better answer? He probably supports over 10 people, giving relatives the chance for good food, health care, safe housing, and education that they might not otherwise have. Your salary goes for... So. New attitude. Tip excessively (that means at least £1) and be pleasant or make the damn tea yourself.

About people who work in your home: newbies think that if you don't get on with the person, you should just hire a new one. Old hands know if you don't bond with the first one, it's almost impossible to bond properly with other ones.

And you need to give up the control—let the housecleaner buy the mops, sponges, dustclothes and pails and give you the receipt. You reimburse with a tip. (If you can get them, of course buy eco-friendly cleaners but if there is a choice, let the housecleaner choose.)

In addition to good wages, bottles of water, and control over when they work, what gardeners usually want is a part of the garden to grow vegetables. Most gardeners are good at their job and not only know how, but like, to work with plants and having to just work with plants the 'madame' choose is no fun, so I always take him with me to the garden store to let him pick out plants and give him a section of the garden as "your choice." That means a variety of vegetables that he grows and takes home with him, fine with me. If he doesn't want aphids on his eggplants, he will make sure there are not aphids on my gardenias.

It's all very 1800s at times when my housecleaner bends down to touch my feet or grabs my hand to kiss it, but I know the second I am out the door, she will be putting her own clothes in the washing machine, moving the rugs, forgetting to dust the fans, and breaking clay pots. It's a balance—from my part: fair wages and no yelling, from them: pretty much whatever they feel like doing. No man is a hero to his valet—no valet is a hero to his employer. We are all human so it's best just to get on with it.

Part 2: It's Not Your Money and it's Not About the Money

Tosha Silver's *It's Not Your Money* is a brilliant book. It's the anti-*The Secret*. She knows the true mystery of the universe: you are not in change. So go ahead and visualize, write fake checks, make vision/action boards, and say affirmations, but along the way, let go of what the outcome is because you aren't really in charge.

In other words: You need people around you who say, "No."

Medieval kings had fools so there was a safety valve,

someone to say the truth amongst all the people who were afraid of getting their head cut off if they told the king he had a stupid plan. I know you are not a king (you are a princess diva) but you need this concept. I hand my tailor a beautiful piece of fabric and explain my dream dress. "No, that is not nice coming, this fabric is not good." I sputter, I plead, and to no avail—he is a tailor with principles. It will not do, so it shall not be done.

I buy a magnificent rose and hand it over to my gardener. He shakes his head, purses his lips. "No." "But the COLOR!" I protest. Head shake. The rose gets donated to a friend.

Of course you have to watch out for people who thwart for the sake of thwarting—but you are a diva, so you are ALWAYS pleasant, hence there should be no need for a person to be athwart you, unless it's a troll and you should know the wily ways of trolls and avoid them.

Surround yourself with good people and listen to them. Respect their sense of pride, their craftsmanship, and the fact that they have important aspects of their lives which are more important than you are getting that cup of tea *this second* or having the petunias weeded *right now*.

Trolls kiss up and shout down—they are super nice to those above them in the pecking order and are unkind to those below them. That's why they have bad breath and meager 401Ks/ISAs. Be nice to everyone, be generous to a fault, and retire early to enchanting Greek islands.

"Can I…"—"No"—Take a deep breath. It's good not to get everything you want.

Part 3: Do It Yourself

A dear friend once called in a panic, she was hosting a

dinner that evening and the two palms in her yard had straggling fronds but the gardener was MIA. "Pull them down yourself," I said. "But I don't know how," she wailed.

Sigh.

Yes another reason why I hate *The Secret*—all that emphasis on thinking of the future and not enough on learning how to use long-handled pruners.

It is truly delightful to have someone clean my house—but I also know how it clean it. I love my tailor dearly and I can tack a hem, sew a button, and stitch up a small rip. Basics, my dear, basics. Let's not throw caution to the wind and learn how to bias cut, let's leave that to the professionals, but get to an elementary standard. Learn how to clean a toilet and, if you have a gardener, pull weeds and water now and then. Get good at tossing slugs (take a leaf from the fig tree, carefully pick up the slug and toss it over the garden wall, also works for caterpillars but be careful because some can cause a rash, use two fig leaves).

Divas are not strangers to machetes (which is why divas so seldom go to jail when an abusive husband suddenly goes missing, but that it the story for another day). I have, more than once my dear, taken on an unkempt date palm and emerged victorious (avoiding being cut by pricks, such a helpful life-skill).

"Don't ask anyone to do what you can't do yourself" is a nice motto but a little ambitious. I would suggest, "remember karma." Now and then, get your own cup of tea. There's a pecking order in the universe and it changes. While you might be able to boss around your tea assistant now, when the CEO calls you in, well... do you want her to treat you the same way you treat the tea assistant?

When people are bastards, be *surprised* because you have never treated your housecleaner, tailor, gardener, tea assis-

tant, waitress, counter clerk or 'customer service representa-
tive' with anything less than courteous honesty.

Give grace—give forgiveness—give patience (and
occasionally practice with machete because one never
knows, does one? 'One,' of course, does not include me. I
know.)

THE SERVANT PROBLEM AND THE MADAME PROBLEM

Ineptitude and pure hatred are hard to tell apart at close quarters. The pipes under the kitchen sink disintegrated, and while fixing them, my plumber decided it was time to clean the water tank on the roof. He drained all the water and cleaned it by scraping off all the calcium deposits on the side of the tank. He hauled most of the pieces out of the tank, but a fair amount was left and when he filled the tank up again, there was quite a bit of calcium free-floating in the water supply. Do you know what happens when you take a shower in water super-saturated with free-floating calcium?

I didn't before but now I do. Ouch. Real Ouch. Did he mean to do that? Did he not know what would happen? Did he just forget to tell me to let the water run for a LONG time before I took a shower?

Or my cleaning ladies. One would move all the small rugs into different rooms. The first time I moved them all back. Next time she cleaned, they were randomly dispersed all over the house again. I pointed this out and asked her to keep the rugs in the same rooms. Come home after she has cleaned to the same scatter-shot result. Point this out again, she starts to cry and hit her head, "Madame, I am so sorry, Madame I am no remember." Ack. I grab her hand, "No, no, it's ok, just please keep the rugs in the same room." Come home the next time—rugs all over the house.

Then there was the time she decided to 'clean' one of the large rugs outside, running the garden hose over it and scouring it with a steel wire brush. Then there was the time

I came home to find she had broken the washing machine. Ok, no big deal, machines break. But the motor had broken and yet there were THREE loads of sopping wet laundry on the floor. She had put a load in, the agitator didn't work, so she took that load out, and put in another load and got it wet. Twice. Does she hate me or was she hoping that if she kept getting the laundry wet, somehow it would start working?

If your cleaning lady walked up to you and announced, "Madame, I am finding those, too big, husband and wife, I am beating too much, too big, children coming, beating, I am beating too much"—what do you think she would be talking about? Turns out she meant monster spiders. She had found two of them tucked in the outside window frame and killed them.

I don't think it was actually a married couple (spider priests? mated for life like swans?) but the amusing part is that when I first found spiders in my house, I talked to Luxchman, my gardener, who blamed "the trees" so we trimmed all the trees close to the house. When I found the next few spiders, I talked to my cleaning lady who swore they came up through the drains (open drains in kitchen and bathrooms) so I bought drain covers. Then the carpenter who dropped by to work on the screen door told me they come through windows. Did any of them actually have an honest idea or were they pulling my leg?

I have to call the plumber for the fourth time because one of the toilets is still leaking. I calmly say, "I want this fixed." There is a silence on the phone.

"Fixed, Madame?" he asks, as if he wanted to be quite sure of my intentions.

"Yes, fixed." More silence.

Resignation, and a little horror, "But that will be costing."

Determined, grim in fact, "Yes, I will pay."

Very well if Madame is so foolish as to actually give money to have a working toilet—who is he to interfere with destiny?

He agrees to come and we set the time at 1pm. I pick him up and he putzs for an hour (not actually fixing anything) then he announces what we will need to buy to repair the parts. OK, but now it is 2pm so all shops are closed until 3:30, and he lives ½ hour away, i.e. if I take him home, I will pretty much turn around to go get him again. And 2pm is nap-time in Salalah. So he announces he will 'stay outside' (it's about 110 degrees).

I say, "Are you going to sleep?"

He doesn't answer, which means 'yes.'

So I show him the majlis (living room with mat/cushions on the floor with AC) and tell him to rest there. So he sleeps in the majlis and I go to sleep in my bedroom—a little weird but he's Hindi, older and I've known him over three years. At 3:30 we both get up and go to the store, or he goes to the store and I sit in the car while he comes out and asks me if I want "Chinese, Italian, or German?" I say, "German!" He is shocked at the frivolous wasting of money to buy a part that might actually work, but he accedes. We go back home, I give him a bottle of water, and go read on the couch. He finishes an hour later. Did he mean to take an entire afternoon to fix a toilet? Are toilets that complicated? How could I tell?

A person I know wrote an e-mail about how difficult it was to get a fake fireplace installed in America. Hmmm. My mom sent me lovely white cotton curtains, sewn with a loop of fabric at the top, to hang from a curtain rod. I show the curtains and curtain rod to the inestimable Luxchman, my handy man, and explain that I want the curtain rod hung above the window. I leave the room. I return to find him nailing the curtains to the wall. I explain curtain rod concept again—put one of the curtains through the rod, demonstrating and explaining. I leave. I return home to find that he has pushed rusty iron hooks THROUGH the curtains and nailed hooks to the wall. Also, the 2 long (side) pieces are in the middle and short (middle) pieces on the sides. So you can't see out the window but have a perfect view of the wall. I walk around the house muttering, "He hasn't seen his wife and two daughters for two years and he makes $150 a month, do not be a mean expat twit."

When I had an extravagant case of food poisoning and was in bed for two days, the first day it was raining so Luxchman painted the trellis, filling the house with noxious paint fumes. The second he cleared the leaves off the roof (THUMP THUMP THUMP). When I realized I had no yoghurt left, I gave him an empty container and some money and asked him to get me "same-same." He has a bike (which I gave him) and the store is about a block away. An hour later (!) he rang the bell, I crawled to the kitchen to see a beaming Luxchman holding 38 individual containers of yoghurt. He had been to every shop in a one mile radius. I thanked him and put it all in the fridge—did he think I needed to take a bath in yoghurt?

There was the time I came home and the cleaning lady said with a smile, "Madame, machine fire!" Hmmm, am I supposed to be happy about this? Is this a good thing, she is smiling after all, or should I be worried? I stroll around the house nonchalantly, looking for burn marks, nothing. Then, after she has left, I found the cremated remains of the vacuum cleaner outside in the garden. How can you burn a vacuum cleaner? Was it in the garden pre- or post-fire? Do I really want to know? No.

She comes in the morning about the time I leave for work—we exchange hellos, then I go. One day I came home and found the kitchen hadn't been cleaned and her purse was still on the counter. Now, no problem if she had to leave and didn't clean, but no way would she leave without her purse, which meant she was still in the house (7 hours later). This made no sense at all. I called her name—no answer and I suddenly realized the only way she would still be in my house was if she had died suddenly. So I stood in my kitchen and thought, oh no, I have to go walk around and find her. I wanted to just call the police but thought that would not be fair, this was my responsibility. So off I go to walk around the house with a terrible, terrible feeling of dread.

But she wasn't there. Turns out, she was cleaning the outside chairs when I had left that morning and I, trying to be nice, had brought her purse (which was outside on the steps) inside and then, not thinking, had locked the door behind me. So I locked her purse, with the key to my house, key to her house and her cell phone inside my house, which she couldn't get to. Poor woman. She had to take a taxi, which she couldn't pay for, to a friend's house and wait until I got home. When she called me that night (from her husband's phone) I had to grovel my apologies.

Did she think that was payback for the rugs, the washing machine, the vacuum cleaner, or did she think I was just stupid?

RUNNING ERRANDS

Most articles I have read about the Middle East are from a position of authority—interviews with leaders, a discussion of empirical evidence, someone in the thick of things, reports from war zones, or scenes of disasters. But there is so much daily life, quiet normal life which never seems to make it into the papers. I ask friends, what are you up to today? Running errands, yeah me too.

I walk into a grocery store. I say 'hi' to the woman who sells watches and Mona, a cashier who has decided to adopt me, buy four boxes of peach tea (you have to horde when you find something you like) and Praise the Lord, they have Diet Mountain Dew after 7 months. Buy 12. Get fruit, bread, and sandwich bags. Go to the check-out. Darn it, Mona has gone on break so I am stuck with one of the regular cashiers who are, hands down, the most unpleasant group of women on the planet. I can't figure out why they are so mean, but they refuse to look at you or acknowledge you in anyway, carrying on chatting with friends (both in person and on the phone) while they leisurely pick up one item at a time, wave it a few times in front of the scanner, then hurl it down to the expat man who is setting each item into its own little bag. I have to walk down and ride herd on them. I can't bag them myself, the guys get tetchy, but if I am not vigilant I can end up with 13 different bags for 17 items. The packer guy pushes the cart with my bags to my car and loads them in. I give him a small tip.

I pull up to my dry cleaners and peer through the plate glass window. The guy comes out to my car with my dry cleaning. I pay him (with a tip for walking to the car) and give him another small pile to clean. All of my clothes and towels are now marked "219" as that was my house number when I first moved here.

I go to cushion guy to pick up the 6 pillows I gave him to put foam forms into. He has found, all on his own, 2 gold sparkle tassels with the same color blue as one big cushion. Would Madame like to purchase the tassels and have them attached to the cushion? But of course. I sit and read while he puts them on. Who can possibly have enough tassels?

I go to my tailor to pick up a purple party dress. I drive up to his shop and peer in through the window. He sees me and waves, so I park and go in. The dress is light silvery lilac, copied from a photo of a dress I saw in *Town and Country*, with a pleated front, band waist and HUGE box pleated skirt, total frippery. Give me access to inexpensive raw silk and a tailor and it's all a beautiful bouffant candy-colored world!

Go to another grocery store; it's tiny but has expat basics like cheddar cheese and marshmallows. Then to a third store for baked beans, muffin mix, potpourri, and light bulbs. No one grocery store has all the stuff you need so it's usual to go to 2 or 3 in a row.

Lastly, I need a new brake light bulb. This would normally mean going to car parts store, buying a new one and replacing it myself or calling a repair place, asking 'if can I stop by' or making an appointment. But it's all different here. First of all, I can't remember when my car place is open. It closes in the afternoon like most shops—but the times are all different. Is it closed 12:30 to 2:30, 2 to 4, or 1 to 3:30? I call my car guy on his cell phone. He doesn't answer. I call the place—no answer, but that doesn't mean it is closed. Perhaps the receptionist doesn't feel like answering the phone. I call 5 times and finally someone picks up. I explain what I need; the guy promises me he will call me back in 10 minutes.

Decision time—of course he will not call me back, but do I drive 25 minutes to the repair shop in the hopes that they will be able to fix it or wait for another day? I decide to go for it. I drive over, park and walk inside. When the guy sees me, he picks up the phone and says, "I am now calling you!" As he has a customer in front of him, we both know he is lying, but no problem. I walk around the counter and sit down next to him. The customer laughs; I open a newspaper and start reading. Ten minutes later, he is free. I explain again what I need. He takes my keys and walks outside. One minute later, he is back to ask me to get in the car and push the pedal so he can figure out which brake light.

I do that, then go back to reading. After another ten minutes, another guy comes in and asks me to come push the brake pedal. That done, he disappears, I read. Ten minutes later he comes back. I go outside to push the brake pedal again. He disappears and I read. Twenty minutes later he comes back with a small box. Outside again to push the brake pedal, then I read.

He comes in and gives the box to the guy behind the counter. I read. Ten minutes later the guy tells me it is $3. I give him the money and go back to reading. He makes out the bill, prints it and gives me a copy. I am all set to go.

Errands accomplished!

HOW TO EXPAT

DARLING, THIS SECTION SETS YOU STRAIGHT about the necessities of life overseas: a butler, a lovely garden, a canvas tent, a good doctor and tips on how to survive drinking volcanically hot tea with the British and Antarctically cold tea with Americans. Which is to say, these are my requirements, yours will be different. But heed the essays carefully because the key is to figure out the things you want and then try all ways that are not morally or lawfully indefensible to attain them. I wanted a canvas tent, something devoutly to be wished for by few people, and yet, verily it was my desire and verily I schemed, plotted and worked for it, as you should for those things which will make your heart sing. You should also celebrate people who do their jobs with kindness and try to understand the cultural norms of odd foreign people, like Americans.

NAMASKAR JEEVES: TALES OF ME AND MY BUTLER IN THE MIDDLE EAST

BLAME IT ON WAY TOO MANY BRITISH NOVELS AT AN IMPRESSIONABLE AGE, I HAVE ALWAYS WANTED A BUTLER, A REAL BUTLER—A JEEVES, A CRICHTON, A GODFREY, A HOBSON, A LANE, A MERRIMAN, A PASSEPARTOUT—TO ANSWER THE DOOR. Someone to screen calls, to take care of the hoi polloi, to be ready with the hot toddy, the crushing bon mot for annoying people, a withering repartee when I am feeling sorry for myself, and an umbrella for rainy days. Someone nicely pressed who, on bad days when everything is hopeless, makes remarks such as "when I was in Lord Balveer's service and all the elephants came down with scurvy at the same time the saffron crop failed, I found it helpful to..."

What I got was Luxchman: medium height, thin, polite, from Kerala, India. I met him when I was looking for a place to live. A local friend had taken me to a 'compound,' a collection of eight villas set four on each side of a small lane with a wall around each house. Luxchman was the manager. He showed us the house and then we stood outside to talk details. He looked so serious, I was thinking of not taking the house—I didn't want to have to deal with a grumpy manager every time there was a problem. Suddenly he smiled, a warm, kind happy smile and I agreed to take the house.

I moved some stuff a few days later and then moved in two weeks later. Luxchman was everywhere, fixing everything, "No problem, Madame, tomorrow coming." We made a deal for him to sweep my garden, water the plants, and wash my car every morning for about $50 a month but he quickly became much more than that.

He was my comrade in arms to make the garden grow from a collection of scraggily trees and weeds to a veritable paradise. He brought plants, moved plants, made suggestions, and would occasionally put his foot down. "No, Madame, not nice coming!" It was that ability to say no to me which made us friends. Most worker guys will simply agree to bad schemes or say yes but then not do the work. Luxchman had a sense of pride—he was not going to do something he didn't agree with. He was simply not going to plant a tree where he thought a tree should not go.

Living alone there are so many times you need one more pair of hands and instead of bribing friends, Luxchman became that pair of hands to help me move the sofa, hang the picture, change light bulbs for the ceiling lights, and hang curtains. When I wanted to decorate the outdoor trellis with Christmas lights, I held the ladder for him and he draped. He held the ladder for me when I trimmed the guava tree. He painted the trellis, kept the front hedge under control, went to town to pay the electric bill and took down the dead date palm fronds.

I started to take him with me to the nursery and the hardware stores to help me pick out stuff. When we walked into one paint store, the men at the counter called out, "Hello Luxchman" and I got a glimpse of how he had a whole other life I knew nothing about. On one of those trips to get cement, two men from a store came out and started screaming at him. I drove up to them and honked. Luxchman got in the car—then I rolled down my window and asked what the problem was. The Indian store owner started to explain that Luxchman owed them money.

"How much?" I asked.

It was only about $12 and so I went into full "Madame" mode—"What?" I yelled, "You are yelling at him for 4 riyal? What is this behavior? DO NOT YELL AT LUXCHMAN! YOU ARE NOT ALLOWED TO YELL AT LUXCHMAN!"

One of the men kept screaming, past me, at Luxchman.

I hollered back, "You are NOT ALLOWED TO YELL AT LUXCHMAN."

He gave up and apologized. I gave him his money. Luxchman stayed quiet. As we drove away, I said, "Not good men!" He laughed. I wish I could have asked him what the whole fuss was about—but we don't have a language in common.

The language barrier means we have had a few mistakes over the years. "Trim" is not a word he understands. "Little cutting" doesn't get through either. He has killed several plants by his radical pruning. He pointed out the right 'outside' paint for the driveway edging that I bought and that flaked off within days. While painting the living room he left a wavy line between the top of the wall and the ceiling which causes people to wonder "Is your ceiling crooked?" Sometimes he leaves and forgets that the hose is running, creating huge pools in the backyard.

But what can I do? He is the one and only Luxchman. It is impossible to get angry. Even when he built me the world's worst garden shed. And when the metal gate got stuck because the metal guide to help the gate slide back and forth broke, he took a pick ax to the wall. Then he stuck the metal guide back in with new cement. But he didn't have it quite level, so it fell out again, with large chunks of cement. Then he did it again, but in the wrong place. More pick ax work, more cement. The wall looks like it was attacked by zombies. But he is the one and only Luxchman.

When I find a caterpillar munching my grapefruit tree leaves, he gets me an almond tree leaf to pick it up with and then, when I toss it over the wall into my neighbor's garden, he giggles, "No nice people, hee hee hee." My partner in crime.

When I ask him to lay some cement garden tiles, I come back two hours later to find they are perfectly set in beautiful white gravel. Where did this gravel come from? Perhaps one of the building sites near my house? Don't ask—don't tell.

I plant chili plants for him and he has free reign to take whatever figs, pomegranates, bananas, and limes he wants. When I saw an odd plant growing next to the jasmine, I asked him to take it out. He said, "No, nice coming." I left it alone. A few weeks later, it turned out this was an eggplant he put in for himself. What could I do? He planted another one and now I have two huge eggplants in my garden. If it makes him happy, it makes me happy. He gets his monthly salary, tips, cold drinks, and whatever I think he might need (towels, my old sofa, a new jacket in the winter) and whatever he asks for (clothes to clean the car, a shovel, new paintbrushes). He used to drink from the hose, but I started to buy a box of water (12 1½ liter bottles) and leave it in the shed for him. I check it now and then and when he is down to one or two bottles, I buy another box.

He now comes two nights a week and one weekend morning to water and clean the garden. When he arrives, I walk outside and say hello. He giggles. I ask him how he is and he giggles. He knocks on the door when he is done—I hand him a small tip if I have the cash on hand, 2 7-Ups, cupcakes if I have been to the bakery, and an empty bag to carry his eggplants home in. He smiles. I smile. I say

"Thank you, good night!" He says, "Thank you, good night, namaskar!" I say, "Namaskar." He pulls back my metal gate, pushes his bike through, closes the gate, and bicycles home. Sometimes what you get is better than you think it will be.

EAST OF EDEN: A GARDEN IN THE MIDDLE EAST

"THIS IS RED GUAVA," THE MAN SAID WITH SPECIAL EMPHASIS. "Red!," he repeated.

I looked at him, his t-shirt mostly covered by a large, grimy towel wrapped around his shoulders, his sarong practically touching his dirt-covered flip-flops.

"Red," I said solemnly, as if I understood the significance.

"Red," he repeated, nodding slowly, letting me in on one of the more important secrets of the universe.

We both stared at the twig rooted in the little black plastic bag he was holding.

"Red, yes, well that would be lovely!" I finally said, judging I had treated the matter with enough careful consideration.

"Grafted!" he whispered. Now that I had acceded, he could come clean.

"Well, yes of course! Grafted!" I answered. I was sweltering in my modest, long sleeved sweater and skirt, my toes browning in the dirt floor of the green-net-covered nursery but I knew better than to try to hurry the transaction.

He nodded and set the guava in the middle of the walkway for one of the 'boys' to come carry it to my car, "and?"

"Two bananas, please."

We slowly walk to the banana tree section.

"Red bananas!" he says, pointing to a plant about 2 feet high.

I stifle my sigh, and we go through another reiteration of

"red!"

I long to say that I don't know or care what the importance of red guavas or bananas is. I am living in a rental house with a three-year contract. I don't think I will see any of the fruit produced by the trees I am buying and even if the trees do manage to create crops, of whatever color, the results will be eaten by birds or my gardener, whoever gets there first.

"My gardener" sounds rather pompous, but in the small town where I live, there is a vast difference between what things sound like and what things are. "My gardener" is the inestimable Luxchman, from Kerala in Southern India. He bicycles to my "villa," a freestanding cement block house with a wall around it, every other day and waters the garden we have created. He also helps me hang pictures, digs holes, gives advice, and generally keeps me on the straight and narrow path of righteousness, except when he steals things.

I met Luxchman when I moved from a small apartment into a 'villa complex' several years ago. There were eight villas, four on each side of a little lane, surrounded by a seven foot wall and each garden separated by a low, three-foot wall. The inside was dire, with industrial carpet and low ceilings, but the garden surrounding the house was heaven. There were two large bougainvilleas which covered the trellis over the sliding glass doors from the living room. At the front was a small 'carpet' of grass (very rare in this part of the world) several large guava trees, hibiscus, and various unknown green bushy things.

The side yard was packed dirt with a few plants in a row by the side wall. The back garden had a large old guava tree, mature hibiscus bushes, and a lime tree. To the far side were the two old bougainvilleas.

An excellent start and, since I never had a garden before,

I thought I just needed to maintain what was there. Luxchman—thin, polite, about 45 years old—was the manager of the complex. It was usual to pay him about $50 a month for him to water the plants and clean your car every morning.

So we started slowly, I bought a few bags of peat moss and tried to resurrect the clay soil in the two flower beds. Then I realized some of the big green bushy things were a noxious smelling weed—well, obviously they had to go. Then I had gaps in the green borders by the wall—that had to be solved. So I found two gardening stores. I got gloves and some seeds. Then, after watching Luxchman drag the hose between the two spigots, I got a new hose. Then the old hose broke, so another new hose.

Any gardener knows what is coming next—the slippery slope. A few more bags of peat moss. Setting up a compost pile. Seedlings. Buying secateurs. Two small lime trees, replanting, discussions at the nursery about whether this shrub needed "sun coming," "too much sun coming," or "no sun coming."

Then my mother came. My mother who, with her husband, turned over an acre of rapacious knotweed near their house into a small municipal garden, complete with stone benches, rock walls, oak and pine trees, and masses of blooming flowers: butterfly bush, yarrow, echinacea, lavender, cosmos and more. She sweetly badgered the town authority into installing a water spigot and hand-watered the whole area.

I would have sworn I had none of her genes when I moved into the villa, but blood will tell. And blood will make you pay $50 to buy a tall ladder to prune the guava trees. She explained that the plants needed to have rocks set around them, so she spent half her vacation with her knees in my clay soil creating garden paths and transplanting aloe vera and canna lilies.

She left and I was in charge of the seeds: morning glories, 4 o'clocks, carnations, asters, cosmos, red chilies, parsley, dill, thyme, basil. Then more plants from the nursery: gardenias, four different kinds of jasmine, roses, a grapefruit tree, various large frond ferns in big clay pots, more hibiscus, oleander and, luxury beyond luxury, three olive trees.

Luxchman would be completely forgiven for viewing my mania with fear or loathing—more plants for him to water. But he was right there with me, bringing small banana plants, frangipani cuttings as big as baseball bats and arguing about placement. "No, Madame, there no nice coming, here, too much nice coming." Soon Luxchman and I were making dates for big projects: driving to a construction site and borrowing piles of small football-sized rocks to line the garden beds and him getting up on the high back wall to trim back the tamarind and lime trees with me holding the ladder. I started taking him with me to the nursery to help me pick out plants.

We would have conversations mixing Hindi, English and Arabic: "*Jumma*, coming, yes? I am *khana* bringing!" meant for him to come on Friday to work for a few hours and I would have food for him, in addition to his monthly wage and tips. When the weather got cold (e.g. 65 degrees) I bought him a jacket. Although this was my first garden, I already knew the most basic rule—your garden is only as good as the person who waters it.

One day I was working on my computer in the living room, I realized something was shaking the bougainvillea tree. I went outside, stood on a chair and looked over the wall—municipal workers were hacking my plants which were spilling over the back wall. There was a dirt road behind the wall, but the plants weren't impeding the roadway. Someone must have giving orders for a 'clean' wall and they were obeying.

Luxchman was sweeping the lane with a palm frond so I jumped into my car, drove up to him and asked him to get in. As I drove off, I realized that I hadn't said where we were going (to talk to the workers) or when we would be back (five minutes), he simply set down the broom and got in. He trusted me entirely and whatever was ahead of him, he was unconcerned, In old pants, flip flops, paint-spattered long sleeved shirt, his rickety cell phone—he was ready for anything.

I drove around to the back side of my wall and pointed out the five men whacking at the lovely long bougainvillea branches. He went over to the workers calmly but implacably. A long conversation resulted, eventually involving ten men. (I stayed in the car—as a single women in the Middle East, you learn very early which battles to fight yourself and which ones to ask someone to fight for you). He prevailed. The bougainvillea remained uncut, a bright mass of pink and green.

When he went back to Kerala for his mandated two month vacation, given every two years, he brought his nephew to work for me—but it wasn't the same at all. The nephew was a better weeder and cut the hedges in perfect straight lines. But he wasn't as friendly as Luxchman, not as interested in the plants.

Luxchman came back and we walked around the garden once a week discussing what was "nice coming" and what was "no nice." He took the chili peppers and guavas as they came ripe and 7-Up was a permanent occupant of my shopping list. I even started to sneak to the empty house next door for a little stealth gardening, cutting back the pomegranate trees, pulling up the wild mint bushes and trimming the baby date palm tree.

Then I got an eviction notice. Panic and consternation! The rental firm was relentless. And lying. They said they needed the houses for "eight engineers" who were coming to work for the company but the real reason was filthy lucre. In the two other compounds owned by the company, they had served eviction notices, changed the carpet, and rented the houses again at double the rent.

I, sadly bowing to fate, started to look for a new place. Of course, now it was mandatory that I have a garden, but villas with gardens were so rare as to be almost impossible to find. Most houses in town are surrounded by a wall for privacy, but the area inside the wall was always tiled or paved for cars or for children to play. I went to see houses with concrete yards in growing despair.

Finally, one week before I was supposed to be gone, I found a likely house. It was not too old and—joy of all joys—had a dirt yard. One spindly fig tree, one overgrown lime tree, a short neem tree, five straggly pomegranate trees and a plethora of weeds in the front yard. Another spindly pomegranate on one side of the house, a green bushy something on the other side (lopsided from being eaten by camels), and in the back yard, more spindly pomegranates, a henna tree, and weeds. By the front door were two large empty raised garden beds and in the middle of the yard a pickup load of dumped dirt and a load of dumped white gravel.

The house was fine, small with a living room for men, an open area for women to sit, two bedrooms, a kitchen and three bathrooms. I barely looked at the inside but checked the lime tree carefully to see if it had limes on it. Limes in abundance. So I agreed to a three-year contract. Then I brought Luxchman to see it. He agreed that it would be "nice coming."

Two days later, he brought three other men and we spent the morning digging up 55 plants. On moving day, my belongings took one truck load—my plants took another. The moving men thought I was insane as they, grumbling, hoisted pot after pot off the truck and put it where I marked out the beds in the dirt.

The next Friday Luxchman, other men he knew and I set out beds, replanted, and hauled rocks to make more borders. Two days later, the first sandstorm of the season hit—the hibiscus, oleander, roses, olive trees, little bougainvilleas, ferns, gardenias and jasmines bent disconsolate. Even the aloe veras looked wane. My previous villa was surrounded by houses and a palm tree farm; this villa was on the edge of town—open to all the winds which blew incessantly, covering everything with a thick layer of sand. After three days Luxchman and I surveyed the damage. "Coming, *mafi mushkala*, coming," he said gamely as he watered the twigs, almost stripped of leaves. During this time, Luxchman changed from being the manager of my previous villa complex to taking care of another set of villas, but he continued to 'free-lance' work for me.

The following week we had the next disaster. I opened my *bab* (sliding metal gate) and drove off, leaving the gate open. Theft is almost unknown in my town so I was not worried about the plants and all my gardening supplies, including buckets, shovels, rakes, and a new wheelbarrow. I was right about the gardening tools—but I forgot about the camels.

Camels wander openly in my part of town. Every camel is branded and owned by someone; they are very social animals and stay together during the day and are herded home at dusk, falling sedately into long nose-to-tail lines. During the day, they forage for food, sometimes leaning over the high walls around houses to munch on whatever is growing in the yard. Leaving the gate open was a kind invitation to dinner. I got back after dark, so I didn't realize the damage until the next day when, walking out of the house I was faced with a scene of garden carnage.

The mango tree was pulled up by its roots; the guava tree was a stump as big as my thumb. Almost everything was chewed, stepped on, or pulled up. Emergency phone call to Luxchman and we spent the afternoon trying to repair the damage. Then the second sand storm came, lasting three days. When the wind stopped, I cut back as much as I could and we concentrated on getting the beds dug, the gravel hauled outside the wall, and some garden paths made. Then the third sand-storm hit.

I lay on the sofa listening to the wind howl, softly repeating, "You can't fight Mother Nature." The wind finally stopped and Luxchman and I went to the nursery near my house to get some replacement plants. We planted another lime tree, pulled out some of the pomegranates and I started asking around for coconut palms.

The government, in an effort to promote gardening, has a free give-away of small plants at the municipal nursery once a week. I borrowed a friend's husband, put on my most modest clothes, and made a raid. Smiling brilliantly I explained my new garden and the horrors wrought by three awful sandstorms. The man in charge was all sympathy—instead of ten plants, the normal limit, I got 22: bougain-villea, oleander and hibiscus all about a foot tall, some spiky ferns and three different kinds of purple, bell-shaped flowers.

We put them in the ground, watered and rock-bordered. Then the fourth sandstorm hit. As the wind was lashing the fronds to bits, I was gnashing my teeth for three days. Another afternoon of surveying the damage.

Then somehow, day by day, week by week—roots took hold, leaves unfurled, buds turned into huge masses of pink flowers. The oleander jumped up to four feet tall—filling out all along the front wall. The roses spread spiky branches in every direction and bloomed. The bougainvillea turned into pink basketball-sized pompoms. The olive trees looked positively Italian in exuberance. The pomegranate trees, severely trimmed to destragle them, put out dozens of day-glow orange flowers. The fig tree took on a proper tree shape and rewarded us with many sweet figs. The lime tree kept up a steady production of limes. The guava twig took off and grew to three feet. The neem tree grew tall enough to shade the driveway.

The side yard now has a long narrow garden bed anchored with one pomegranate tree and enhanced with many different purple flowers which no one knows the names of. The backyard holds a stately procession of trees: almond, a short palm of some kind, henna, grapefruit, pomegranate, banana, orange, pomegranate, banana and coconut. There is a compost heap and sturdy, barbed aloe veras.

The Indian jasmine by the front steps kept up a slow procession of blooms, the filled-in raised garden beds have mint, out-of-control purple asters, recovering garde-nias, unstoppable 4 o'clocks, feathery cosmos, and giant sunflowers, lower leaves torn by the storms but continuing up to six feet tall. The ferns in their pots settled down.

It was time for larceny. Luxchman came to water the garden one night and started to explain something—which takes a long time given I know 5 Hindi words and he knows 25 English words. I finally figured out that he had somehow found a pile of garden tiles which are being thrown out and "too many people taking." He thought I should drive him there, to load up my car with tiles to make garden paths. How sweet and how typical of him, sacrificing his own time to help me make my garden. So I put my jeans and a sweatshirt on, we pop in the car and drive all the way to the other side of town, where the municipality is tearing up the tiled area in the middle of a divided highway to put in flowers. It's 8pm, there are cars going by on either side of us and the stack to tiles, supposedly on offer, are under a streetlight.

I am torn. Are we really going to steal town property in the middle of a busy road? Why yes, he is. Luxchman jumps out and loads up the back of the car with sang-froid. When he finishes, I put the car in 'drive' and I realize that these are not just garden tiles; they appear to be lead-reinforced concrete garden tiles. The hood is lifted up from all the weight in the back and I can barely get the car to move. We drive home at 25 miles an hour, me terrified that the tires will blow. We unload the car and all is well.

The next time he comes to water, he makes it clear he wants us to go get more tiles. I agree, heck, larceny is my middle name. When I come out of the house after changing clothes, he is sitting on the steps fussing with his flip-flops. He already busted one pair a week ago and I gave him one of my pairs. But now at least I have a way to repay him for putting the tiles in the car. We stop off at the cash machine, then I drive to one of the big stores in town, give him money and tell him to buy himself shoes, while I sit in the car and read. Then we go steal more tiles.

On one of the days when the tiles were still piled up in the driveway waiting for the weekend for Luxchman and one of his friends to put them in, I ran into one of my old neighbors. She told me, somewhat nervous as to my reaction, that the garden in my previous villa has been completely destroyed. The manager of the villas decided that the plants were interfering with the whitewash on the garden walls and ordered everything cut down. The old bougainvillea was cut back and then torn up by its roots. The old hibiscus, 15 feet tall, was cut down, the jasmine which reached up to the roof was gone, as were all the plants in the flower beds, the banana plants, the lime tree, the hedges, the lilies, the roses, even the aloe vera I had left behind were all pulled up and thrown out.

She looked at me closely—was I going to cry or rage? I shrugged. As they say in the Middle East, this is the life. When Luxchman found out from his friends what happened, he came to me stating indignantly, "This no good man! All going! All cutting! No good man!"

I agreed. What could we do? I remembered one of my favorite stories from a college art history class. A tale about how there was a rare snowfall in Florence and Michel-angelo's patron asked him to make a snowman. What a wonder—the world's best sculptor creating a masterpiece in snow.

Plants grow and die. You make a garden and it all disap-pears. So it's gone—but while it was there Luxchman, the birds, frogs, worms, crickets, and I really enjoyed it. I don't have time to figure out what circle of hell the company that owned the villa is going to—I have to go buy some 7-up and cupcakes (the preferred *khana*). There is an empty space next to the fig tree and I am thinking, maybe a guava would be happy there. Red, pink, purple—the color doesn't matter.

A TENT AND THE PINK
CARDIGAN OF DOOM

A FRIEND MENTIONED SHE HAD CAUGHT *OUT OF AFRICA* ON CABLE TV. She gushed about the acting—Meryl Streep and Robert Redford—the story, the pathos, the glory. All I could think about was the tents. Those totally fabulous, metal-framed, canvas-colored canvas tents with tie lines and little overhanging flaps. Tents with camp beds and folding stools. Tents with rough leather bags scattered on the floor and proper trunks with thick leather handles. Tents which say, "Let's run over to Kilimanjaro," "Fancy a dash over to Bobo Dioulasso?" "Shall we scurry up to Cairo for the winter hols?" and "The Kalahari is charming this time of year." The tents spoke British, with nary a flip-flop or six-pack or laptop or GPS in sight. The tents said, "If you can't find your way with a conventional paper map, twenty years out of date, stay home."

I seriously love those tents, and have yearned for one ever since. The accompanying elephants, camels, or guy with a bi-plane might be hard to find, but I was sure if I managed to get my paws on one of those tents, that paraphernalia would show up on their own. I got my first love (a Land Rover) by cunning and a pink cardigan within 6 months in-country; the tent took another four years but was worth the wait.

Some people love the place where they were born. I think they are the lucky people, like someone who decides at five he wants to be a fireman and grows up to become a fireman. Yves St. Laurent crying at four years old because he didn't like the buttons on his blazer. Lucky. Most people thrash about for awhile, trying different jobs, trying different places until they either find the right spot or settle. A friend loved Alaska, fell in love with a girl from Arkansas. They moved to Pennsylvania.

I occasionally ask people who have known me for a long time: Did you see this coming? The rugs, the draped fabric, the intense desire to shop in souqs, the longing for a crusader castle of my very own? Where does the fevered wish for a moat come from? I have loved perfume, scented soaps, and frou-frou stuff since childhood and have been tossing scarves over chairs and tables for years, but the ornate gilt frames, the colored glass lanterns, the decorated glass candle holders, wind chimes, bamboo mats with silk and gold borders, and thinking Versailles is slightly under-decorated—how did all that get into my DNA?

My mother was a Pueblo Indian in a former life, she doesn't really believe in owning anything except pottery and books. My father is all about modern style, sleek designs, less is more. Hah. More is more—strands of beads hanging from the stairwell, saris draped over the banister, fake plants, painted wooden cupboards, blue and white Iranian print bedspreads, and pillows. Dozens of pillows, pillows in heaps. I have about 150 cushion covers, none very expensive but it takes me two days to change my pillow color scheme every season.

I am the woman who buys the fake tiger skin rugs; I am the one who piles rugs on top of rugs. When I first saw over-decorated gilt furniture in Cairo, I practically wept from joy. I refer to the main Jim Thompson store in Bangkok as "the mother ship." I want one of those Syrian living room sets of six monumental chairs with inlaid mother-of-pearl. I want Moroccan tile tables.

I can turn any room into a French boudoir, cat house, seraglio, with red velvet curtains, heavy perfume, collections of small brass objects grouped on pressed metal trays on ornate little metal tables. I have plinths. Who do you know with plinths scattered around the house? I have garlands of fake flowers, red lacquer trays holding bottles of perfume and shells and a huge spray of fake jasmine branches in the kitchen, decorated with lavender glitter hearts and silver bells. I buy metallic gold paint by the gallon. I drape costume jewelry on drawer pulls and cupboard handles. Do not stand between me and a display of scarves. I will squash you like a bug.

But still the tent was calling—that little room of happiness to put on the flat roof of my villa was out there in my future, waiting for me. And when it was time, I pounced. Using the appropriate Middle Eastern non-linear method, I tell my plumber, who I have known for 3 years and who speaks good English, that I want someone to come build a steel framework for me. Off he hies to the 'workshop' area of town, a few days later he appears with the metal guy and two assistants. They take measurements and argue the price. The plumber is the middle-man. He says first the price is 200, but if I want "A class," it will be 250. They argue in Hindi, the price comes down to 230. I say that I will have to think about it. When I call the plumber two days later, I say I want 225; he says it will be 215. We both know when the guy is giving a lower price than you offer to pay, that you know you have not bargained enough. But on the other hand, if you leave a little 'sugar' in the deal, you leave the way open for the beginning of a beautiful friendship. The metal guy has a good price, which means I have the right to complain if something is not as I want it. And the plumber is in the middle to smooth things over, for which he will get an honorarium.

After a week, the plumber called: the tent was ready for inspection. I went to the store, called "Metal Workshop," one of five stores with the exact same name in a line. The grey metal frame was standing forlorn in the work court-yard, looking like a home for camel fodder, not my dreams. First, green paint! And then, spying some leftover decorations in a corner, I ask him to add some metal flowers sprayed with gilt to the corners, take off the metal door and raise the roof line. Leaving 'sugar' in the deal, means I don't have to pay more for the little flowers. Then I ordered my 'fire pit,' a round BBQ (with detachable grill!) on tall curved legs so I could make tea on the roof.

The next week the tent was delivered and I got a worker guy to haul concrete blocks up the roof. The metal frame was perfect, 5 by 5 meters, the edges were about seven feet tall, and the center bar was 9 feet off the ground. The BBQ pit was a disaster, he had made a metal cauldron about 5 inches off the ground—way too deep, legs too short—so we had a long discussion about that.

Then time for plywood for the floor base. I had gone to the building supply place twice before to scout plywood prices, but this time was to buy. Sure, they avowed, they would be happy to sell me the plywood but I would need to arrange my own truck as it was after 5pm, the drivers for hire had all gone home and they could not let the store's driver take my stuff.

It would appear to be an impasse but I am wearing the pink cardigan of doom. If a woman ever asked me for advice about moving to the Middle East, I would tell her: get a baby pink cardigan with mother-of-pearl shell buttons. It works wonders. To segue for just for a moment, Westerners who have never been to the Middle East like to harangue me about how sexist the Middle East is. This is not an argument I want to get into because it's like trying to explain Dante to iguanas, but one brief remark—you can sometimes use the sexism to your advantage. Some Americans take this to mean, "wear a bikini and get what you want," and like almost all American thinking about the Middle East, it is the wrong attitude. Correct thinking: pink cardigan.

So when the building supply guys started in about how it was not their responsibility to get the plywood to my house, I smiled serenely ensconced in my pink cardigan of doom. Their doom. No way could they win this argument. They were going to deliver the plywood to my house—like it or not.

"Go behind that grocery store and rent a truck yourself," said one guy.

Ha ha ha. "Do you think I will drive up and ask some men to come to my house?"

Silence. Discussion in Hindi. "We can't help you, Madame." I sigh, and settle into the chair. Discussion in Hindi. "Madame," one man pleaded. I sigh, and settle further into the chair. They concede and agree to deliver the plywood to my house.

Then there was the matter of getting it up onto the roof. Here, they held firm, one of them starting "Madame! We are a building supply store! It is not our responsibility..." I held up one manicured finger and said, "Stop." He stopped and let me cognate. Now I needed someone to take the plywood up, but who and how? Dearest of all dear people, Luxchman my gardener and I might be able to do it, but I would get hot and sweaty and he is getting on, with a game leg. It would be better to get some young worker guys. But how do I find some to come to my house? I sincerely adore Luxchman but we don't have a language in common. Aha! Solution!

I dial Luxchman and request the clerk to ask Luxchman

in Hindi to bring two strong worker guys to carry things when Luxchman comes to water the garden that night. He agrees, Luxchman agrees and I dash off to the smithery to get the hopefully improved BBQ. The BBQ is so fabulous, I want to cry. The guy simply cut the cauldron in two, so there was one shallow octagon basin on short legs, and then a perfect 'wok' shaped piece on tall legs, big enough so I could make a small fire to warm a tea kettle, cook kebabs and toast marshmallows.

Back home, Luxchman and the worker guys come. They haul up the plywood. I explain clearly what I want and then leave them alone for ten minutes. I come back and find they have put everything in the wrong place. Explain again. Leave. Come back after ten minutes to find everything is in a new, but still wrong, place.

This is a never-ending philosophical debate about getting work done in the Middle East. My philosophy is "Don't watch, you don't want to know," i.e. explain, leave, come back, explain, and keep your temper. Some people have the "stand and supervise" technique which is time-consuming and demeaning. You end up shrieking like a fishwife, "PUT THAT DOWN! NOT THAT WAY! STOP! OVER THERE!" I can't bear it.

My other technique is to do something while they are working, not that I can help workers. I have given up on that, but to have them see me do something creates, in my point of view, a more natural atmosphere. Less 'Madame and the boys,' more 'we're all in this together.' Better than money, 7-Up and thanks is the chance to see a Madame do something that they can laugh at. So as they arrange the concrete blocks and maneuver the plywood sheets on top, I hang curtains around the sides of the tent frame, put them up, realize they are the wrong way round, put them up again, decide I don't like that color there, take them down, put them up again. Then I get the clay pots with jasmine bushes into position and put the BBQ in the front corner.

Once the plywood is in position, I put down the padding rolls, then the plastic mats, then pillows, then cushions, then the little metal-scroll work table, a dozen tea lights, the little white metal bookcase to hold the tea supplies, the leopard-print fleece throws, the gold sparkle scarves, and the colored glass lantern to hang from the center beam. A tent of dreams. Happy happy happy happy. Now I am just waiting for the guy with the bi-plane.

THE SLOW-DOCTOR
MOVEMENT:
PROPER BEDSIDE
MANNER EXPLICATED

I LOATHE AMERICAN-STYLE DOCTORS. Most seem cranky, superior, condescending, unpleasant, and harried, always harried. Ok, they are usually right—that's a benefit but their behavior.... The one who sat staring at his computer while he asked me questions, typing in the answers. The one who snapped, "Look it up on the internet" in answer to my question. The ones, several of them, who watched impassively while I cried. The one who, when I mentioned his diagnosis was opposite to the diagnosis I had received the day before, shrugged. Being given acupuncture in a freezing cold, storage closet, then left alone for half an hour. When the doctor came back and found me crying and shivering, she announced, "Some people find acupuncture helpful."

Ah, but Indian doctors in the Middle East. That, my friends, is where it is at. That's who you want and need, oh so desperately, when you are not feeling well, when the pain seems to have no cause and no end.

The basic question is what do you want: brutal competence or kindness? Do you want some white coat, fantastically fit, to breeze into the room where you have been waiting, freezing, in a paper-thin robe which doesn't fit, hurl a few questions at you, poke you in much the same manner as you treat a Thanksgiving turkey, pronounce (without justification) an answer, scrawl out a prescription and dash away? Do you want someone who has ten minutes, and only ten minutes, to spend on you, most of that time spent reading your chart? Do you want someone to whom you are a 'case,' who 'presents' with certain symptoms?

Or do you want to be a person? With a name, a real name? When I got bit by a scorpion, the nurses at the hospital crowded around with questions, not questions that had anything to do with my medical history, but where I was from, was I married, where did I work, how long I had been in town, did I like it here, was I happy—annoying and yet comforting. I was not 'presenting with scorpion bite.' I was a person who fit into the life of the nurses and the life of my town.

I still remember the first time I went to a doctor in the Middle East. I showed up at the hospital, paid a small fee and a nurse motioned me to go in the room. And there was the doctor, sitting at her desk, waiting for me with a weary smile. I handed her the folder with my information, she tossed it down without looking at it.

"How are you?" she asked. "How are you?" was there ever an American-style doctor who asked me that? "What's wrong?" perhaps, but the normal procedure is to read the file, then ask for clarification. This doctor asked several more questions, gradually getting to the point of my visit.

And she was tired as, I eventually learned, all of the Indian doctors I have seen in the Middle East are. This sounds rather odd, to want an exhausted doctor. But American-style doctors usually bounce into the room Tigger-esque, work frenetically, then bounce out. Imagine a slow doctor, a quiet doctor, one who has the time to sip some tea while talking to you. One who looks world-weary, as if your pain is not some personal failing to live up to a Puritan ideal of health, but part of the general malaise of the world.

Indian doctors in the Middle East all look like they know children are dying of cholera while I am moaning on about some insignificant complaint. But they are stuck listening to me instead of doing real work. I find that very comforting, as if, no matter if I ended up with gout, leprosy, TB, malaria and dropsy all at once, they had seen worse not one hour before. American-style doctors look at me as if I am the ten-minute interruption between them writing an article for *The Lancet* and their squash game.

I had an x-ray that showed an abnormality. Unfortunately I was in a hospital at the time with an American-style doctor. I asked her what showed in the x-ray and she, full of energy, snapped, "You will need to make an appointment with the surgeon. He can see you in about a month." Not exactly the reaction you would want. "But what is it," I asked, "What is the problem?"

"All over the world doctors are not reading x-rays!" she barked.

Oh so comforting. Spent a sleepless and terrified night in hotel room, got back to home and straight to my tired, Indian, homeopathic doctor.

When I walk into his office, he slowly stands up and smiles sweetly, "Oh, it is you! How are you?"

I hand him the x-rays and he puts them down on his desk without looking at them, then, "What is wrong?"

Words! Communication! Exchange! I explain, then he opens the envelope, checks the x-rays and the written report. First words out his mouth, "You are ok." My blood pressure sinks 20 points.

He explains all the medical terminology, what is going on. When I say I want to see a medical doctor as well, he recommends someone and explains how to get to her clinic. I take my homeopathic medicine and drive over to the clinic.

At reception, I register for the clinic, pay $9 consultation visit fee, get a little ticket with a number and go to her office. My number is on display, so I walk right in. She is sitting at her desk, looking tired. I hand her my chart and the x-rays. She sets them on her desk without opening them. We chat. She opens the envelope, checks the x-rays and the written report. She calls the surgeon and they both agree I am fine. We chat for a while longer. No time pressure, no pronouncements from on high, no bouncing, no dashing. People talk about the slow-food movement; I want to start the slow-doctor movement.

How to Behave with Americans and English

	Americans	English
When in doubt give them	Tea with lots of ice	Very hot tea
Do not try to understand this unfathomable summer drink	Sweet Tea	Pimm's Cup
In conversation—1	Understand that it is impossible to have a real conversation. The rest of the world thinks "Let's meet for coffee" means two or more hours of talking. To Americans it means they arrive 10-15 minutes late because of "traffic" or "they were busy"; then they tell you how busy they were, are and will be. If, by chance, during the conversation one of you happens to mention any fact or question (who directed Casablanca, when the Washington team won the Superbowl, the name of Rembrandt's mother or what are the ingredients of Clafoutis, etc.) out must come the electronic device to check the answer-that very moment. Americans cannot bear to live with the uncertainty and are unable to speak until they know the utterly useless fact which will be instantly forgotten.	Not to worry—unless they met you in kindergarten, they want to have sex with you, or it's a business meeting, they won't talk to you. Ever.

	Americans	English
When in doubt give them	Tea with lots of ice	Very hot tea
Do not try to understand this unfathomable summer drink	Sweet Tea	Pimm's Cup
In conversation—1	Understand that it is impossible to have a real conversation. The rest of the world thinks "Let's meet for coffee" means two or more hours of talking. To Americans it means they arrive 10-15 minutes late because of "traffic" or "they were busy"; then they tell you how busy they were, are and will be. If, by chance, during the conversation one of you happens to mention any fact or question (who directed Casablanca, when the Washington team won the Superbowl, the name of Rembrandt's mother or what are the ingredients of Clafoutis, etc.) out must come the electronic device to check the answer that very moment. Americans cannot bear to live with the uncertainty and are unable to speak until they know the utterly useless fact which will be instantly forgotten.	Not to worry—unless they met you in kindergarten, they want to have sex with you or it's a business meeting, they won't talk to you. Ever.

	Americans	English
In conversation—2	Deal with the smiling—all statements from "I saw a wombat yesterday" to "It appears a tidal wave is crashing down on us" will be accompanied by a big smile and you will be viewed as evil if you do not smile constantly. Buy teeth whitener and practice a lot.	Deal with their refusal to smile. Ever.
Navigating	Don't believe anything they say about directions. Americans can't maneuver more than 2 blocks from their house on their own. Everyone uses GPS devices that are often wrong or broken. There are only 10 Americans left who can navigate by dead reckoning and they are kept in a special zoo in Nebraska. You can visit them and give them peanuts; everyone else, when they tell you how to get anywhere, nod in agreement and get there on your own.	You won't understand anything they say about directions, They will either use N-S-E-W instead of right-left, they will give you longitude and latitude or they will use incomprehensible landmarks such as "at the furze, turn towards the copse, then go straight until the ha-ha"
Their houses	Don't go to their houses if you have claustrophobia (the houses are crammed with stuff) or lived in the Middle East (the houses have low ceilings, bad rugs, pets and a lamentable lack of marble, gilt, frippery and boxes of Kleenex). Warning: some kitchens are decorated with wallpaper featuring duck with bow-ties. Don't look—Don't ask.	Ditto. Warning: their bathrooms are teeny-tiny. Warning: There are usually a lot of photos around. Never say anything like, "Oh, there's a photo of your grandmother and the Hungarian Olympic shot-put team," it will inevitably be a photo of the person and her bridesmaids. Stay silent.

	Americans	English
When you are a guest	Hosts act like waiters. You walk in and they say, "Are you hungry?" If you say, "No," you will never get any food. Ever. If you say "Yes" they will start in on, "Do you want black tea or green tea or chamomile tea or filter coffee or instant coffee or Coke or orange juice with pulp or..." Whatever you say, you will get more questions: "Do you want full fat milk, skim milk, soy milk or almond milk? White sugar, medium brown sugar, dark brown sugar, or icing sugar? Do you want that in a cup or a glass?..." The only way to survive is to bury your fear and break in with "Cold water in a medium sized blue glass."	There are no questions—you will get tea and whatever they feel like giving you and you will eat all it. Or else.

HOW TO TRAVEL

DARLING, THIS SECTION IS A VERY REALISTIC guide to travelling unlike so much that is written for people trying to see Peru on $10 a day or those reading *Town and Country* (rent this fey bungalow for $5,000 a night). I, as you well know, am quite the realistic one and am here to help you voyage when you have more than a pittance and less than a fortune, unless, of course, you start to call yourself a 'nomad' or make nasty remarks about tourists, then I will seize your passport and you can stay home for a few years. Yes, moving about always creates a mismatch of expectations but divas leave the house knowing it is their responsibility, and only theirs, to get what they want. Being aboard means recognizing that while people aren't out to get you, they are also not arranging their life to serve you. The second important point is: go where you want to go. Don't go to Italy when everyone says you have to, go when your heart says you must (even if it is, sigh, Vermont). Avoid anything that even remotely sounds like 'should' and see the things you want to see.

HOTEL—QUACK QUACK

WHEN PARENTS TELL THEIR CHILDREN NOT TO HAVE SEX UNTIL THEY ARE MARRIED OR IN LOVE, THEY SHOULDN'T YAP ON ABOUT MORALITY AND THE BODY IS A TEMPLE AND STAYING "TRUE" TO YOURSELF. They should show their kids one of those old science movies in which baby ducks get imprinted on a hapless person, who the ducks follow everywhere quacking. That's what happens. The first person you sleep with gets stuck in your mind, a quack quack quack that never shuts up. See, you're thinking of yours right now.

If you have been traveling your whole life, you have a certain kind of immunity but for those Americans who head to Europe, South America, or Asia for the first time after they have reached the 'age of reason'—it's duck time for you. The first European hotel I stayed in was an Italian monastery. Huge old grey stones, thick walls like battlements, tall narrow windows overlooking a walled garden, monks in long robes. The person I was traveling with and I had to crawl over the ancient stone garden wall the night we came in late because the front door was locked. Do you think I could possibly come up with something nice to say about a Hilton, Radisson, or Marriott again?

Staying in hotels is like collecting charms on a silver bracelet. Restaurants, guest rooms in other people houses, airports don't have quite the same pull. On boring days, I spin through the memories: The Gasthof in Heidelberg where I stayed on my way to see a friend in Freiberg. I got off the train, found a place and realized, right before I went to sleep that, for the first time in all my 19 years, not a person on Earth knew where I was. The Intercontinental in Al Ain where I discovered I had found a new best friend. The expensive, quaint B&B in Kittery, Maine where I decided that I didn't want to live in Maine. The cramped, hot little room that the man with the policeman hat took me to from the Rome train station. I was sure I was being taken to an underworld den, never to be seen again but it was true: there were people who met trains in Rome and walked tourists to nearby hotels.

The hotel in the Emirates straight from a Graham Greene novel. The little place in Corsica with a bedspread that looked like Cookie Monster had been skinned. The Motel 6 in Minnesota where I found *Star Wars* on the television, which seemed as good as a sign as any that I should move there; the Motel 6 in Freeport, Maine where I crashed after an afternoon of shopping (who knew Clinique had an outlet?).

The immense room in a house in Florence which was at least two hundred years old, tiled floor, all the massive furniture, including the four poster bed in heavy dark wood, but terribly cold. Early spring, no heating, the guy I was with and I simply could not get warm, the perfect metaphor for our relationship. The hotel room in Assisi with the fabulous view, but not even the sight of white doves wheeling in flocks above the dark green trees could bring a St. Francis-like peace. That guy and I were not going to make it as a couple either.

Those German Gasthäuser with impossibly white, impossibly soft cotton comforter covers and fitted bottom sheets. English B&Bs with their tiny breakfast rooms and parsimonious breakfasts. That feeling of peace and contentment when you close the door to your room in a French hotel when you have succeeded in completing the room-renting transaction without mortally insulting the owner, being throw out, challenged to a duel, or had your parentage abused.

You forget the name of the hotel, you would never be able to find it again, the details of the decor escape you—but there they are in your memory. The one in Portugal where I splashed so much water on the floor during my shower that my sister wanted to know where the dolphins were. The one in Rhodes where it was so cold, I had to go ask for extra blankets. I came back and announced to my friend, "I think we are in trouble, the landlord had a woolen hat on, inside." The tiny room in Paris that had walls at eight different angles. The formal living room, almost as big as a ballroom, in Hungary that was turned into a guest room for me, my boyfriend and his brother who hated me, where we got into a fight and he wouldn't come talk to me until his brother fell asleep. The room in Maine where my boyfriend and I stayed for a wedding, which he hoped would make me think of a wedding with him.

Hotels mean transitions—the relationships strengthened or torn apart in hotel rooms. The sleepless nights wishing you were someplace else or with someone else. Sitting on the bed writing postcards, resolutely not calling home, crying, eating a half pound of the best local sweet, and reading trash, studiously ignoring all the things you are supposed to be out seeing. Looking out the window and day-dreaming. Sitting at the desk and studiously planning a complicated itinerary for the next day—only 48 hours allowed for this city and you are going to see all of it.

So off you go now, think about hotel rooms, maybe even head out to one. Just be careful about that first overseas hotel room. It has a fierce power, an unshakable quack.

OUT OF THE WOODS: MAINE

W<small>E ARE NOW GOING TO TALK ABOUT</small> M<small>AINE</small>.

Oh no, you are not going to rag on Maine.

ME? 'Rag on' a place? ME? When have I EVER had an unkind word to say about anyone or anyplace? I am the SOUL, the very personification, of discretion and kindness! Ahem. The best part about going traveling it that you get to see all sorts of places where you never want to live, thus making you infinitely happier with your present domicile. And, by the way, I just got home from Maine.

Maine is a lovely place.

But of course it is. Very lovely. And my family is lovely. I adore my family very much, which is a good thing because I don't understand them at all. With all the large, over-populated cities filled with cafés to vacation in, they chose a cabin in Maine. Yet, as I adore my family, verily will I follow them anywhere. Even to Maine.

You know that feeling you get when you can finally take off your shoes and socks, squish your feet in the sand and walk to the ocean? You don't get that in Maine. Sea, yes. Seacoast, yes. Sand, no. Maine USED to have sand, lots of lovely soft pink sand that was deliciously satiny and the perfect resiliency for beach walking. But the Puritans decided it was too frivolous and they loaded it all on ships, dumped it in the heathen flesh-pots of the Bahamas and brought back loads of sharp, pointy rocks. Thus it is difficult, if not impossible, to get from the roadside to the actual ocean.

But those dedicated Puritans realized it was still possible

to enjoy the ocean, so they sent out the fleet again to lasso icebergs and haul them home until the average ocean temperature was 45 degrees and all the minnows wore little knitted woolen scarves and fin protectors. Then the Puritans ascertained that it was STILL possible to at least get some pleasure from LOOKING at the ocean, so they directed their sails to Africa, used ultra-fine fishing nets to capture swarms of the most virulent, aggressive mosquitoes and set them free along the coast. Surveying the flinty beach, frozen water and hordes of bugs, they shook hands with each other, said 'our task here is done,' and went to work banning the sale of alcohol in the Boston Athenæum.

But hey, beaches are not the only natural attraction which heightens peoples' appreciation of the natural world. Maine has lots of other lovely lures. It has, for example, trees. Lots of trees. Many trees. I hate trees. I hate forests. Looking at a picture of a forest in an air-conditioned room which sipping a well-made martini is a pleasure I would deny no one but to WALK through a forest, to go INTO a forest... never.

Now let's examine this logically. (I am a perfect slavish fiend to logic.) Maine is full of forests. Forests are full of large creatures who want to eat you. No one in the café of a large metropolitan museum wants to eat you. Perfectly clear, yes? And yet people continually ask me, "Darling, want to hike through a primeval forest?" as if "get mauled by mountain lion" was on my 'to-do' list. Or to put it another way—who is the scariest writer in America (besides the twit who writes the *Wall Street Journal* editorials)? Steven King. Where does he live? MAINE. Got it? Could it be any plainer?

When I think of "woods" I think of two life-altering experiences I had. One was the summer after I graduated high school and was on a (forced) walk up a mountain in Glacier National Park. We were walking along a path through high grass with lots of berry bushes as it was explained to me that this time and place (August amidst berry bushes) was exactly the right time and place to see bears. Up Close. Very Up Close. As the furry dears would be so enamored of lolling in the sun eating berries, they wouldn't notice your approach until you were Right Up Next To Them, at which point they would either amble away or eat you. What fun! Traumatize yours truly on her summer vacation! I was petrified. Petrified I tell you. So petrified that TO THIS DAY I am afraid of bears. I live in urban splendor and I still think, "ok, now if I hear a bear snuffling about in the hallway, I go out the window."

Do you know what I think is bold and fearless? Ordering Vietnamese coffee in a café for which I don't have a complete, written assurance that they know how to do proper Vietnamese coffee. When I feel quite the giddy daredevil, I go pick up my dry cleaning without first putting on makeup and perfume.

I mean this in the nicest possible way: we are not related.

The second forest experience was in Germany. I was spending Christmas at a cousin's whose husband was in the military. They rented a small house on the edge of the Black Forest. Cue scary music. So on Christmas Day I decided to take a wee stroll in the snow on the path that went by their house and straight into the forest. For the first ten minutes I was congratulating myself on how very 'outdoorsy' I was, walking along this narrow, dark path in the snow which muffled everything, surrounded completely by tall, ancient trees. Then I realized that it would be very easy to believe in elves in such a quiet, mystical place. Then I realized it would be very easy to believe in goblins, trolls, haunts, and cougars in such a place. I was so desperately frightened, and for no particular reason, that I turned around and walked back and have never willingly gone forest walking again. I'd rather drink sub-standard coffee than put myself in feeding range of a leopard.

But the woods are dark and deep.

Dark and deep indeed, and full of creatures who view you as an ambulatory snack. When I think "Appalachian Trail," it's as if someone sidled up to the wolves and whispered, "You know, if you just go over towards that path, there's always something yummy for lunch." Imagine you're a hungry jackal, lounging on a tree branch and there, strolling along singing Pete Seeger songs and wearing half the L.L. Bean catalog comes a hearty soul—fingers for appetizers, assorted organs for main course, a leg to take away for a midnight snack. I think the whole walk-in-the-woods thing was STARTED by a carnivore consortium; all the little wolverines paying PR companies fees to get their habitat written up as prime camping locations in *Down East* and *Outside*. Do you know there are whole colonies of badgers (smart animals) who make a living by altering tree stumps to look like park ranger signs, directing clueless day-hikers into bobcat territory?

Now picture yourself in a nice, safe, happy desert. What can hurt you? The sun, if you were dumb enough not to wear a hat and sunscreen. But there are no ticks, no poison ivy, poison oak, poison sumac, poison crab-grass, poison birch trees, no mosquitoes, no deer flies.

But darling, rats, tarantulas, snakes, cockroaches, centipedes, scorpions hold no terrors for you.

Yes, but a) they are all Greta Gaborish and want to be left alone. You only see them when you move the rock they are hiding under; c) they are all smaller than me; and c) none of those animals see me as a major food group.

And if you aren't in a forest in Maine, you are in a B&B in Maine.

You are going to complain about B&Bs? We can't take you anywhere.

B&Bs are run by people with three characteristics: 1) They like to be awake in the morning, and by morning, I mean before noon. 2) They like to talk to people in the morning. 3) They are insane. Which leads to a fourth characteristic: they like to talk to you IN THE MORNING about the people who stayed at their B&B the day before, so that you know that TOMORROW morning, you are going to be the topic of conversation for the next round of guests. Thus it is VERY early in the morning, say 9 am, and you are expected to 1) speak and 2) say something that will be memorable for the next day's guests. This is utterly beyond my facilities – pressure to perform at 9am is simply too much for a fragile blossom like me.

I don't know how you got into this family.

In addition, this particular hypothetical B&B in Maine was vegetarian. Vegetarian as in, run by a woman who wanted to give you the genealogy of your granola, as in "this milk is from Mabel, our four-year old Guernsey. Now, she had a collapsed udder last winter, but it's a little better now, you have to tug a little harder but you rub it with a rosemary and pig-dropping compress and it heals right up, but that foot rot is still a problem. You'll be able to tell from the taste that she got herself into the nettle patch last week, but what's a little extra vitamin D in the milk? Now the butter is from Daisy, our five-year old Holstein..." I doze off briefly. "The pancakes are made from whole-wheat organic flour, hand strewn by Verurula Stevens who lives down the road six miles in the blue frame house which was made by her great-grandfather with beams he..." When I wake up again she is asking me, pointedly, would I like spinach, kale, cauliflower, or beet in my omelet. Now if she had just put a spinach and feta omelet in front of me, I would have eaten it. I have eaten a spinach and feta omelet once of my own volition. But it was served to me by a non-earnest person who slapped it on my plate, said "eat something green, it won't kill you," then gave me a Bloody Mary. Not someone in homespun, standing at her kitchen door with a look in her eyes which said, "I bet you put refined white sugar on your Cocoa Puffs and swill it down with non-union beer."

Now that look in her eye, combined with the fact that it was 9 am and anything I said would be repeated the next day, made me answer the "What do you want in your omelet" question with: "M&Ms."

In self-defense I must remind you that I was totally unprepared for such a question—they never ask such things at the Ritz. There it is always "Darling, would you like a Bellini or a Mimosa, or shall I just bring three of each as usual?"

Fine. If you are going to be like that, you can just stay home next summer.

VEGAS VEGAS VEGAS

BASICALLY YOUR EVIL INNER CHILD IS WAITING FOR YOU IN VEGAS—THE PART OF YOU THAT WANTS TO DRINK BEER (NO PAPER BAG!) while slouching down the street and puffing on cigars while walking around indoors. The only men in suits were casino management or grooms. It is the last American refuge of people who want to smoke cigarettes while using public restrooms (ashtrays in the bathroom stalls!). There are no curfews and no clocks (only one I saw was the trademark one on the Tiffany store) and no need for effort—moving sidewalks, escalators, elevators take you to the next (well sign-posted) attraction.

Oh yes, your evil inner child will revel in the 'tasteful' topless shows, the all-you-can-eat dinners, the REO Speedwagon songs drifting through the air and the Siberian white tigers. Your allergies will disappear because all the plants are plastic; you can go see any former star in concert without irony. Attempting to fit in, I tried to get us to go to "The Thunder Down Under"—Australian male dancers (ONLY because I have an Australian character in one of my books and wanted to take notes on their accents and common expressions. They ONLY take their clothes off to better express their emotional turmoil at being so far from home.) But even though her daughters were safely at her sister's house and the man in her life was hundreds of miles away, Zita, my friend who I traveled with, wanted to go to the Guggenheim art exhibit, the aquarium, and a re-creation of a medieval tournament. I adore Zita but she doesn't really understand the sacrifices necessary for quality book research.

It's not that you CAN loaf about—they want you to—

loafing is positively encouraged. Unbutton your shirt to your navel and fluff out your chest hair! Wear that orange-and-black-striped stretch crop top and camouflage pedal pushers! No Euro-trash here, just swarm after swarm of honest Americans enjoying their constitutional right to dress like 4-year-olds in public. Every male from 4 to 84 in long, baggy shorts (who started this trend? can I slap him?), t-shirts and sneakers—they come loitering down the walkways crumpled and wrinkled as shar-peis.

So you would know what dens of iniquity to avoid, I kept careful notes but it appears someone spilled a Bellini on them, making them illegible but I want you to know, Zita and I SACRIFICED ourselves for you, constantly stopping ourselves from having fun to scribble notes so that YOU, the reader, would have the FULL benefit of our accumulated wisdom. I would NEVER think of going someplace as garish as Vegas for my OWN pleasure.

Dear readers, we did not selfishly sit in overstuffed cardinal-red velvet chairs at little white marble tables and drink pink cocktails with 11 ingredients placed on white linen coasters for our own benefit—we did it to gain the energy to continue to explore (we ate every meal in a different hotel) only for your sake.

You can only talk about Vegas in a sarcastic tone, but since I can't get out of bed without being sarcastic, it's easy for me. Vegas is a deliberate 'anti-place.' It's there to remind you of other places that you can't get to or don't want to go to, like Medieval England or Egypt, but because it has to squish everything together you get the (originally female) sphinx with King Tut's face and a store featuring Native Americans in your fake Norman castle (as Zita says, "Native Americans are an important, but little known, part of the English Middle Ages").

I liked Vegas because it reminded me of places I know (i.e. the Caribbean with palm trees, warm, sunny, ringed by mountains, and the Middle East with all the white or silver cars that are very clean). But the aesthetics aren't as impressive—not enough gilt (although even the police are trying, they have shiny gold helmets), not big enough chandeliers, the duct work and vents aren't hidden well enough—but there are immense, air-conditioned spaces that neither overwhelm nor amaze, like that hotel in Abu Dhabi with huge, empty open halls and vending machines from which you can buy gold bars.

The older hotels are situated in their specific location—they are set right next to the sidewalk and have little balconies. You can imagine people sitting outside, looking at the mountains, watching the street life below and drinking a lot of cheap beer. All the new hotels are set back at least a block from the main road (so they have moving walkways to get you from the street to the inside) and could be designed for any city, any country. For example, the coolest take-home present has nothing to do with Vegas: go to the M&M store and get a little baggie of M&M's in all sorts of colors that they never sell in the regular packages. Zita took some home for her girls, made sugar cookies, spread them with white frosting, explained the concept of "mosaics," and let the girls make mosaic cookies, but then very few of us can be Zita.

Each of these new hotels has a theme, with two or three "attractions" and several restaurants. At least two of the restaurants are in keeping with the theme (pirates, Italy, Paris...) and the rest are some combination of fake Mexican cantina, fake Italian trattoria, fake French café, fake English pub, fake sushi bar, fake Chinese—unexpectedly there was no Canadian cuisine to be found anywhere.

Thus the "Venetian" one has two (count them TWO) fake canals with fake gondolas being fake driven by blond gondoliers singing 15 seconds of opera arias. They also have an art collection borrowed from the Guggenheim and a mini-Madame Tussauds. One of the many reasons why it is fun to travel with Zita is that she can quote like a fiend—when we went by Madame T's she said "He is a man of wax," which we ALL know is from *Romeo and Juliet*, she even knew the SCENE it was said in. Later that day she managed to slip in T.S. Eliot. When I complained that there were camel figures in the "Treasure Island" theme hotel, she said it was a "mixed metaphor." Later when we saw a most unlikely looking bridal couple, she said, "See, another mixed metaphor." Yes, she's a good one with a quip, inspecting an ersatz Roman colonnade, she said, "Ah, all the classical styles at once."

One sad aspect about Vegas is all the brides, we saw about seven a day. A woman in a floor-length white gown with veil was wandering around the lobby as we checked in at 1 am; she was alone and holding a plastic bottle of soda. The other sad aspect is the gambling. There is a slot machine for every passion—I Love New York, *I Dream of Jeannie*, gold mining, bass fishing, Little Red Riding Hood, vampires, diamonds, *The Price is Right*, Texas, zodiac signs, unicorns, Italy, *Hawaii 5-0*, dolphins—you just walk around until you find the "right" one for you. (We assiduously gambled 50 cents each day—Zita came out $5 ahead. I lost every time.) At the card tables, Asian women deal to white frat boys (young and not young); crowds at the craps tables were more mixed, couples, all races and ages. I don't understand why people don't just walk up to the nearest hotel employee and hand over a few hundred dollars at the beginning of their stay, seems like that would be less painful. Zita said that of all the gambling she has seen and all the gamblers she has known, only THREE made money at it. Lots of grandparents at the gaming tables. My grandma read me *Anne of Green Gables* and had cats; I am very, very lucky.

It is like the Middle East in that you are constantly aware of a lot of people who are barely getting by who make everything happen for you—bringing you more coffee, selling you postcards, taking your ticket for the roller coaster ride, selling you chocolates from Maxim's de Paris—but for people in the Middle East, often their wages could buy them businesses and houses and a high level of security because it gave them a much higher standard of living then where they were from. The woman I went to at the salon was saving for her own salon in the Philippines, the woman who cleaned my house was saving for an apartment of her own in India, etc. But the people who are working near the poverty line in Vegas have few opportunities to get out.

Zita, who used to deal poker in Montana (which I think is about as romantic and exciting a job as one could possibly have), says that the whole casino/hotel business is quite feudal. One can look at Vegas hotel/casinos as a series of 'castles' owned by lords, tended by an innumerable number of serfs: busboys, bellhops, the people who service the slot machines, clean the craps tables, refill the platters at the buffets, wash the sheets, tune the air-conditioners, dust the plastic plants (which emit canned bird songs), make sure the aquariums get de-mucked. They don't make much money but get a sort of reflected glow for being associated with "their" hotel.

Lots of people like Vegas (the air is so still I counted 14 airplane trails across the sky at one time) but although I was glad I went to see it—I would only go back as a way to see Zita. I know it's silly to say "Oh I wish I had seen it before" but I think I would have liked Vegas a lot better back when it was sleazy and you sat on your balcony, looked at the mountains (instead of other casino high-rises), drank beer, thought tough thoughts, and looked at real gamblers (not your grandparents!), real bad guys (who would never dream of wearing baggy shorts), and women of questionable repute (what complements scenery better than a few women of questionable repute?). It would have been my kind of place, I would have worn pink lamé with a feather boa and lost a few thou after a steak dinner and before going to hear Frank sing. Now it's got no teeth and no shimmer—the Mall of America-West.

On the flight home from Vegas, I sat next to an Elvis impersonator which seemed appropriate. Vegas is a theme-park impersonating a town.

MALTA

Malta rates TWO essays. The other essay, which I will write shortly, includes a subtle yet effective history of the island; vital information on flora, fauna, mineral deposits and fishing rights; a through ranking of the health food stores; a pictograph of the mountain ranges; a fascinating riff on the impact of the Averginian heresy on coal imports and a chart of the interdenominational factions. Look for it soon.

To begin—have you ever heard of Maltese fashion? Malta style? Did you think that was an oversight of world opinion, that Malta was an undiscovered pearl of splendor and magnificence? Hah. Hah. Hah.

I arrived at the departure gate for my flight and thought, "Oh no, it's going to be another Brindisi." We need to get this over with early. Never have I seen such a collection of seedy and scruffy, not in a rakish/raffish way but a rap sheet/prior conviction way.

On the plane I sat next to nice middle-aged British women, that kind whose husband does something international/technical has lived everywhere, unshockable, tea drinking and you can have those great conversations about how hard it is to get good help in Azerbaijan and lighting fixtures in Abu Dhabi. It is all very 1875s but without the imperialism.

When the plane landed, everyone clapped, then immediately stood up and started to pull things out of the overhead bins—as the plane was still breaking on the runway. Quite amazing. The stewardesses were all fussing over the loudspeakers. Made no impression. About 2/3 of the plane were standing up as we approached the gate.

Airport security were not in uniforms, not so much as an insignia – middle-aged men in middle-aged men kind of sweaters. Same feeling as in the Middle East, you misbehave and they will take you in the back room and beat you to a bloody pulp. Then kill your pet dog. If you really annoy them, they will put your grandmother in a "French sucks" shirt and abandon her in the middle of Montreal.

Western European security regulations are tight, but the people enforcing those regulations are either adenoidal teenagers who spend their whole time flirting and sucking down cokes ("Oh, was that, like, a grenade, oh, whatever"), elderly gentlemen snoozing, and mom-types ("Is that a sawed-off shotgun—no TV for three weeks and you have to baby-sit your sister on Friday night.") Maltese security people are all former drug lord bodyguards who are wanted for questioning by Interpol.

Taxi driver to hotel did not talk. Not one word. Hmmm. In Singapore the guy was racing to tell me every detail about the wonderfulness of Singapore (and evils of the Japanese); London taxi drivers are usually chatty. But the silence gave me time to solidify my first impression of the countryside—a combination of Greece, Italy, France, and Spain—but not as nice as any of them.

Hotel. Of course it was under repair. I can't think of a hotel I have been in lately that either desperately needed a paint job or was in the process of getting a paint job. There is a world-wide reservation network: SHE is coming, break out the jack-hammers. [Exception was Raffles—which had no construction but ruined my breakfast. They are STILL not forgiven. NOT FORGIVEN, RAFFLES!] The room was decorated in dark brown and pumpkin orange and they did that really annoying thing where they put all sorts of mini-bar goodies on the dresser and if you moved them goodies to a drawer or cupboard, they charged you for them because they were no longer "in sight." Cable TV had no movie channel, 4 business news, three cartoons, and the local station. See don't you feel better about staying home?

The hotel was 10% occupied, definitely off-season, which meant no foreigners, which means you get to see more Maltese—not in the sense you have the opportunity to, but that you had to—and while I don't mean to repeat myself or be harsh (as if it was even possible for me to be harsh) but having to see (as in, not having the chance to not see) more Maltese is not a good thing. Did I mention I kept scrawling words like "dingy," "reprobate," and "subterranean" in my daybook? Was Malta ever someone's penal colony? Men look like they all had unsuccessful careers in car theft and the women of all ages had the fashion sense of Madonna, circa "material girl."

You know how you walk down the street in Italy—even in your best clothes and wearing your gold—you want to cry as everyone is so well-attired, so smart, chic and elegant looking, with sleek hair, smooth skin and confidence galore? That doesn't happen here. Awake for 27 hours, wet hair, jeans and a canvas bag and I was still ahead of the game.

Then, of course the shopping district was seven minutes walk away. I hate that. The shopping district is always a bloody seven minutes walk away, which means it is 25 minutes and you get lost twice. Shopping districts should either be part of the hotel or a short taxi drive away, so you can go shopping in fun shoes. When a hotel clerk says, "seven minutes walk," he is really saying, "Ha, ha, you have to wear your sneakers." Brat.

So I go outside, and seeing a few taxi drivers standing by their cabs [looking particularly disreputable, smoking, hunched over in dirty black zip-up jackets and old tennies]

I ask them how much the cab fare is—OOPS. They are guests at the hotel, sorry.

Malta: even the tourists are thuggy

Found the shopping district. OUTDOOR mall. No cafés. First purchase is a jacket—brrr, crisp, low 60s. Got some books. Bookstore had a 68-volume collection of Maltese history, 68 volumes—what could have possibly happened to merit 68 volumes? In a large font it couldn't possibly be worth more than 23 pages. I have spoken. Then for an authentic Maltese meal at the Hard Rock Cafe. Nachos, salad, and a cheeseburger. Oh bliss.

Thought I would be all over the bread, but either the bread was not good or I have lost my taste for it—was all over the LETTUCE. Me, can you imagine? I was eating it with my fingers, kept forgetting you can't do that in public in the west, and stealing it off the food displays.

Breakfast at hotel: four kinds of pork, blackberries, and apple pie (they had sparkling wine but I didn't indulge), paper napkins (sigh) and Andrew Lloyd Webber without words (double sigh), stewed tea (triple sigh), over-baked mini-chocolate croissants (quadruple sigh and a back flip), and the famous Maltese pea-pastry.

Went to main city, Valetta—large, walled city with huge lovely gate—looked promising. But the main fort is called, wait for it... St. Elmo. First, someone needs to look into possible attempts of Jim Hanson to proselytize by naming Muppets after Catholic saints. Second, I can't take a fort seriously, no matter how old and big, that is called "Elmo." Third, although it is huge, ancient, and impressive looking, you can't go inside it except on Sunday afternoons because the Maltese police "NEED" to use it. You know how big the island is? 122 square miles. And the police need a crusader fort to control it? Massive police stupidity? They don't want tourists in there fortsie? Fort is being used for large-scale drug production?

Walked around and then stopped at my first café. A very important step. How well I remember, how I wish I could forget, my first Greek pastry (it was a Tuesday, I was facing southeast): I bit into a slice of fabulously decorated cocoa-chocolate cake to find the cream was fake. The horror. The horror.

Would the Maltese get it right? Were they to be grouped with the southeastern Mediterranean (ok for baklava, never trust a cake) or ascend to the chosen land of "even the cardboard is delicious" Italy? Well.

COLD cappuccino, messy appearance, bad cannoli and an almond macaroon we will not mention.

Walked around more, one main walking street with shops and lots of small streets off to the sides, sloping down to the water. Definitely a place not lawless, but with laws unto themselves, insular, very very "us" versus the tourists. It was all about the money—I got cheated a little every time I bought so much as postcards. They have EIGHT coins in circulation. Every penny counts. But I didn't complain, I mean, sure they were covetous, but it's not like a chemical peel and a new shirt would help them join the human race. Theirs is an integral scruffiness.

They reminded me of stagehands, a sense that this was a party-place—many discos, cafés, gentlemen's clubs, tourists shops that weren't open now—but the place would be packed in the high season with the Maltese carefully extracting maximum profit.

I can't imagine how awful it would be in the heat with MORE people when it already felt overcrowded when I was there, ick. Not many tourists—a few Germans in ostentatiously functional orthopedic shoes. Hate them. (functional shoes that is.)

Walked around more—walled cities are very nice but this felt too crowded and all the views of the water (city is surrounded by water on three sides) showed harbors full of boats. Yet, my radar was working and I managed to find the completely unmarked shop full of Moroccan pottery on the otherwise deserted and shopless street. Hah!

Second café: real cappuccino with cute little flower shape made from powered dark chocolate, horribly weak milk (anemic cows?), good chairs, proper marble tables, profiterole with heretical lemon-flavored custard and too-sweet chocolate sauce, fake whipped cream, mini sweet they gave with cappuccino was dry and burnt. Cannoli had stale nuts, flaky (crossantesque) shell and same heretical lemon-flavored custard filling. I, personally, would nail that custard to a tree and slap the person who made it. Standards, people, standards.

Malta: we learned our manners from pirates and our pastry techniques from indigent bovine

Walked out to the fort, which was nice but, really, I can not count on "Elmo" for anything.

The language is very interesting—a combination of European and Arabic. Number are Arabic, they say 'good morning' in Italian, 'good night' in French etc. Written, it has a lot of the letter 'j' and many apostrophes. I want to know the linage of "triq"—their word for street.

While wandering, decided Malta is like Austria—has the reputation of being small and cutesy but they are a ruthless people, bent on self-preservation at all costs. Only people who I could get to smile were a few middle-aged women who were in obvious sympathy with the electrified rodent that seemed to be hanging on to my head. Epic bad hair days in Malta. I think my hair was trying to blend in.

Went to 5 star hotel, meant to have afternoon tea but when I saw the tearoom I knew they were not to be trusted. I would bet anything it would be stewed tea. And since it was 3:30, decided to have lunch: roast pork with spinach. Yum. I practically licked the plate. Then I went back to hotel and had a massage (yes, jack-hammer going in the next room). That night went to a "wine bar" at nearby hotel and had an antipasto with two glasses of rosé. Then I went swimming in the heated indoor pool.

Next day I got up early and took a bus (Leyland, a BRITISH firm, thank you very much) to an old walled city inland (called Mdina, as in "medina", the Arabic word for "city."). Very much a sense of quiet daily life. Store fronts are uniformly eight feet across and very deep, maybe 40 feet. No heating and very few with A/C—wear the same clothes indoors and out like Greece in the winter. America's contribution to shopping is stores with enough room to swing a giraffe, which are kept at a 40 degree difference from the outside temperature.

Took bus back to main city and, oh look, the "Cafe Royale!" Playing Bee Gees music! Time for today's necessary scientific experimentation. Cappuccino: sloppy presentation but hot and good foam. Tiramisu was in cake form (round shaped, of which we do not entirely approve), more of a nutty flavor than strictly canonical and the cream was a bit more plasticy than we have expressly sanctioned. Almond cookie was not exactly *comme il faut*.

Back on another bus to the northern part of the island.

Palm trees, cactus, green fields with low stone fences—but no vistas. In any direction you could see large, ugly, new buildings—so sense of sweep of landscape (kind of like parts of England where every tiny plot of land is manicured). Very palatable sense that I had come to late, and you know this is not something I say often. I don't moan about how beautiful Nice was before the tourists but Malta must have been amazing about 40 years ago—beautiful limestone buildings from the 1200s to the early 1900s on which you can trace Italian and Arabic influences—but everything modern in concrete and without style. Too many people, tatty shops, packed roads. It Italy and Greece you can get out into the countryside and see hills still covered with trees, orchards or acres of vines without a person in sight but there is no 'scope' in Malta. Claustrophobic.

Looked like parts of Crete but no sense of Greek friendliness and openness. No Homer. No Hector. No Hercules. Kept searching for signs of Italy (Sicily is only 60 miles away) but the driving had no death-defying esprit. No anemones. Olive trees lined some streets but in an unromantic, boring sort of way, as if there were mere linden trees, not heroic, storied, fabled olive trees. No visions of the Apian Way, tree nymphs, marching legions, or passion. The only thing better than Italy was Malta had fatter, sleeker cats.

To another nice hotel for afternoon tea, sigh. Tea in a tea bag, paper napkins, chocolate chips in the scones, oh let's just throw a veil over the whole thing shall we.

Malta: when a good Italian café might be too much joy

Next morning had breakfast in the hotel lobby. A raspberry gateau which would not disgrace a provincial café in France and a cappuccino with a slight liquor flavor to the coffee. Little treat you got with cappuccino was one of those dry, crunchy almond cookies. Only took three days but I finally had a proper snack.

To sum up: the point of civic pride in Malta is doorknockers, often in the shape of dolphins. While I would never suggest a plague and earthquake, if every structure erected after 1939 were to disappear, well, I wouldn't necessarily qualify that as an utter tragedy. If you want the Malta experience in the States, eat some sugared almonds in a biker bar.

ZURICH

THE PROBLEM WITH ZURICH WAS THAT I COULD NOT FIND, TRY AS I MIGHT, A YOUTH HOSTEL. What could be nicer than a lovely youth hostel? Sleeping in the same room as eleven other people is such a great way to get to know new people (or as I say 'friends I haven't met yet'). And you, helpfully, get woken up at 7 a.m. so you don't miss a moment of the day. And you get served a lovely, filling breakfast of happy, healthy oatmeal and weak tea (too much caffeine is not good for you! I always prefer weak tea! Without sugar of course!)

Yes, try as I might, there was not a youth hotel to be found within miles of Zurich. And what is even worse, no B&Bs either. The horror! I love B&Bs, just love them. It's like staying with family! I scorn turn-down service, chocolates on the pillow, anonymous maids who flit in and clean, concierge services, stacks of fluffy white towels and the decadent joy of using a "Lush" bath-bomb full of lavender flowers and rose petals and not having to scrub the tub afterwards. Scorn it, I say. Give me home-spun, simple pleasures and people who want to have a nice long chat with you over breakfast at 7:30 a.m.; the breakfast consisting of oatmeal and weak tea, naturally!

But no, I was denied this happiness and was forced, forced I tell you, I mean practically at gun-point, into one of those small European hotels with fabulous pure cotton sheets, a feather comforter, wooden furniture, mini-chandeliers in the room, a velvet slipper chair, and huge enamel tub. How I suffered! I will spare you the details except to insist again how much I hate central heating: 1) noisy and 2) all the air whooshing about in vents takes the humidity away so your skin gets dry. Dry skin—is there a more important problem in today's society? I don't think so.

This hotel, not to belabor the point, had proper heating—metal radiators so that in the morning I would run 4 inches of scalding water into the tub with a little Dr. Bronners peppermint castille soap and voilà! the air was warm, properly humidified, and with a lovely invigorating scent! In the evening, another 4 inches with a few drops of my perfume and voilà, instantly relaxing atmosphere. I have always thought that with a few hundred dollars and a few days I could turn Alcatraz into a cozy pied-a-deux with a certain decadent air. It's a gift. Why fight it?

Swiss Air did not serve chocolates on the plane which I found startling. Seats were not great, and the video system did not work (boo hiss!) but took off and landed on time.

Swiss customs were perfunctory then suddenly I was in a clean, organized, well-lit hall, very disorienting, especially as there was a large, yellow sign saying "Heidi" with an arrow. I got on the airport train-shuttle and as we hurl along through the tunnel, suddenly you hear cow-bells and cows mooing. Irony. I am not used to irony. Then there is one of those 15-second movies along the wall of the tunnel showing a "Heidi" herding cows and blowing kisses. Swiss sense of humor.

Got to hotel at 6:30 a.m. and they let me into the room right away. Swiss sense of hospitality. Try doing that in USA or England. Went out and about. Had bought LL Bean parka for the cold weather but when I put it on, I could not get the zipper to work. I hadn't zipped a coat closed in three years and unlike riding a bicycle, you can forget how to do it. Took me about ten minutes dancing around and cussing.

Ten minutes later I was out on the street; first purchase,

mittens; second, scarf; third, hat. So very odd to blend in to the crowd; having a bland face really helps a lot. In New Zealand people thought I was a New Zealander; in Norway, they thought I was Norwegian; in Zurich, they thought I was Swiss.

Zurich in winter, even at Christmastime, is very grey which would be annoying long-term but for a few days it was fine. Everyone, as in everyone, had a black or dark grey coat; all the cars were black, rather sinister feel, very early John Le Carré. Plain front buildings in grey and white that make Canadian towns look exuberant. But the restaurants! Oh, the restaurants! I never went into any, but there were dozens with lovely table decorations, candles, starched white heavy linen tablecloths, headwaiters resplendent in suits and junior waiters in waistcoats and silent black shoes, twinkle lights decorating topiaries outside, wine lists, discrete lighting! All the tables were set with water, white wine, red wine, and champagne glasses. So comforting.

I ate in cafés and had a few sausages from stands (sausages! yum!) but you could just tell this is a city that takes dining seriously and does a good job of it.

And yes Virginia, there is a Santa Claus and at Christmastime in Zurich, the people from Lindt chocolates really do stand outside of supermarkets and hand out free chocolates. And the shopping was excellent, not avant-garde, not cutting-edge fashion, nothing loud and nothing tacky—Hannes B. and Ludwig Reiter. As a woman who went to high school in the time of preps, I could appreciate all the plain, simple leather boots; plain, simple cashmere sweaters; plain, simple well-cut camel-hair coats (I have one that would have fit in perfectly. My mother got it for me ages ago and occasionally reminds me that she spent more on that coat than anything she has ever bought for herself. I occasionally remind her there is no use having children if you don't spoil them rotten; it helps develop their character.)

My character, if I do say so myself, is developing nicely. One of the main issues is, naturally, to develop a sense of priorities, which is why I only went inside one church and spent an hour plotting my routes so that I could visit every recommended café, including the café in Hotel zum Storchen, Café zum Opera, and Café Harold. People think cafés are all fun and games, but it is a serious endeavor. You have to know how to get a good seat, order the correct beverage—it's not just cappuccinos! Sometimes you need to try a café Baileys, sometimes the Baba au Rhum. Not to mention fifteen minutes every night making sure your pronunciation of 'café mélange' is correct. I once saw a man say it wrong and the café went dead silent; every face turned from him. He slunk out in shame and misery, reduced to Starbucks for the rest of his benighted existence. It could happen to you. Be careful.

Then there is the judging—wait staff (scale of 1-7 on fifteen different points), atmosphere (scale of 1-9 on 12 aspects)—then you have to review the menu choices, actual food, decoration of food, presentation of food, choice and placement of tables and chairs, space utilization, lighting, ambiance, heating, disguise of heating A/C ducts, quality of other customers, tone, mood, display of liquor bottles, flooring, sound-proofing, respect of integral structural qualities of the building, respect of integral historic qualities of the building, attractiveness of sugar packets and I haven't even mentioned the tabulations for glass wear, table wear, silverware, napkins, tablecloths and waitstaff uniforms.

A few trolls kept asking me, "But you went alone, how

can you do that? You were alone! Weren't you sad? You were all alone!" But if I was with someone they would have forced me to go see something cultural when what I really wanted was to see all (prepare to be fascinated) the 5-star hotels in Zurich. Most are really not that remarkable or elegant, except the Widder which has substituted style for hip/ sleek/modern/cool (literately, they have a bar set up outside in winter, and thus is usually below freezing, that serves only vodkas). All of them had small, cramped, boring lobbies and small uninteresting tea/lobby bars. But what was clear was that the staff are trained to respond to expensive clothes and only expensive clothes. Americans can walk into any hotel in the Middle East or Asia and everyone jumps because they know Americans don't usually show wealth through clothes (i.e. you can't judge annual income by shoes) but if you come to Zurich, you've got to wear your money.

Another lesson is that, as you always suspected, Europeans have nicer childhoods than Americans. Better bread for one. Nutella for two—the Swiss boys next to me on one plane flight spread their croissants with butter and then laid on a thick layer of Nutella, a level of decadence even I cannot countenance. The toy stores are like something out of a dream: hand painted wooden toys and doll house furniture, stuffed toys with personalities, the most fabulous, winsome Noah's Ark sets I have even seen. I wanted to buy one for all the nieces and nephews except they were the same price as diamond earrings.

Another lesson is that, as you always suspected, everyone has nicer department and grocery stores than USA. Everyone. There should be a 'Head-start' program for USA department and grocery stores; it is just ridiculous how lousy USA is in comparison to the rest of the world. We need some sort of World Bank assistance. USA has some

OK (not great) fancy department stores but the staff are condescending and everything is too expensive, or you have someplace like Macy's which is a zoo, nothing is organized, no one can help you, goods all in a heap and long lines at the cashiers. Oh, dear people, the Zurich stores, I mean, shut my mouth and call me Clarence. Not expensive, very lower middle-class prices, fabulous taste, interesting items, helpful sales clerks, no lines, and the grocery stores have EVERYTHING. Fresh bread, beautiful flowers, stuff to make stuff (it so helpful when I am precise!). It's like a Dean & DeLuca's for people on a McDonald's budget.

On the scale of whether Zurich is a good place to be rich, I would say, it is perfect if you are wealthy and sort of boring. Chic is not a word for Zurich. Neither is fascinating. You have very good quality, very expensive things for sale and nice cafés to rest in between purchases. I guess if you want to ski (and note: ski = exercise, so consider yourself warned) there are some mountains nearby (I never saw them, either dark or cloudy). Let's see, Zurich would the perfect place to recover from a face-lift or a bad divorce. A good place for elderly Anglican clergy who have some private funds. Perfect for after that rafting trip down one of the lesser Amazon tributaries or drug-smuggling opium out of Afghanistan. Friendly, calm people although some can be somewhat too accommodating towards dictators, tyrants, and monsters (do not let the whole cowbell/Edelweiss/fondue smokescreen fool you—kindly note that in my hotel room, for the first time in my life, the Bible in the drawer included only the New Testament). Hmmm.

Motto for Switzerland:

Yes, we are nice to every murdering, scum-of-the-earth oppressor,

by hiding their money
But that means we will also be nice to you,
With all of your faults.
In fact,
we wouldn't dream of mentioning your faults,
As in, any of your many many many faults,
So there's no need to get upset.
Here, have a cuckoo clock and a chocolate.
You'll feel better.

PICKING A CITY TO VISIT

DARLING, PEOPLE TALK ABOUT WHEN TO GO CERTAIN PLACES, TAKING INTO ACCOUNT THINGS LIKE THE WEATHER. For example, one is told to go to Paris in the spring. But what is in Paris in the spring? Parisian women who will be wearing amazing clothes, heels, and that French pout. You will look like a toddler in comparison. GO TO PARIS IN THE WINTER. Parisian women will all have red noses and be unable to make charming conversation because their feet are cold. You, in chic-but-warm boots and a bright red wool coat with matching lipstick, will stop traffic. The museums are empty and the hotels are cheap.

But never visit Paris if you are broken-hearted—you will jump in the Seine after seeing attractive couples kissing on every street-corner (the French government gives citizens a tax rebate if you and your petit(e) ami(e) spend one hour per day kissing on street corners to annoy single tourists). When broken-hearted, go to Switzerland. The men, well, shall we say, they look like they work in finance—not the finance like "I got money to burn and I want to spend it on buying you Lamborghinis" but "I would like to have a three hour discussion on reverse mortgages." Your heart is safe in Switzerland, plus it has good chocolate, good wine, lots of cheese-based dishes, and good views. You will recover in Switzerland.

In the spring go to North European countries where the denizens will all be sickly pale white or sun burnt. As they (oddly) often choose to wear white clothes and are tall, there is a definite stork-thing going on. Wear flowered shirts and as much pink as possible.

London is slightly tricky. The men look ridiculous—the

tight pants/huge shoes look flatters no one and you will be giggling over your gin. But UK men have good patter, even the most unattractive has got good lines and can be a very plausible fellow. Best to go when you are in a committed relationship so you can enjoy the silly pick-up lines, with no chance of getting stuck in a sunless country with citizens who can't make a decision without a cup of tea.

Also, never go to London or England if you love British literature. People in British literature are NOTHING like people in Britain, unless you have read only Thomas Hardy.

Places like Amsterdam and Baltimore are safe at all times; there's enough going on that whatever your mood, you will be fine.

Boston—only in the fall. Never in summer (teeming with parents teaching children to hate American history), never in spring (which occurs on three different days between March and June), never in winter (if you want to be cold, be cold someplace with better food and better views, like Bozeman). And remember, the Puritans never died, they just started wearing khakis. Do not be fooled—this is a city to buy practical shoes in. DO NOT get any kind of beauty treatment, these are people who deep down think that beauty is ungodly. DO NOT go to a spa, DO NOT get your hair cut, DO NOT get a facial, DO NOT get anything waxed. If it's an emergency, you can go to Lush (Lush stores are always demilitarized zones) and get soap, but if you buy make-up in Boston, DO NOT come running to me that you look like an 18th century spinster whose entire family died in a whaling accident. You deserve it.

New York—go when you are distracted by something else so the city is merely a backdrop. Trying to look at it is like trying to look at the Grand Canyon—you know you are supposed to feel something but after ten minutes of trying to take in the grandeur, you want an ice cream. Treat New York as a setting for something else and it works— you can only understand New York by looking obliquely.

Chicago—go when you need a mood booster. It's a great place with nice people. They have Frangos and good shopping. And a river. And a lake. Go when you need someplace better than you think it will be. Lots of good food without the pretensions of San Francisco. And no, I am not discussing San Francisco—fog, hills, tech people—I would rather visit Des Moines.

MOVING TO VERMONT

So when and why should you come to Vermont? Native Vermonters don't want you to come at all, except maybe to rent a summer cabin for a week or so and spend a lot of money at "country stores," but no littering, no back-chat and you had better be polite. But let's say you a brave soul and do want to jump into the Vermont ethos—the spirit of place—the mountain Weltanschauung. You should approach Vermont as Ulysses did Ithaca. In fact you should read Cavafy's poem "Ithaca" a few times.

Come to Vermont after... after you have sown your wild oats. After you have enough of global politics and are ready to spend one day a year at the town meeting and six days a year reading your town's booklet. (Do as the natives do—start with reading the list of people who are late with their taxes.) Come after you have pretty much said everything you meant to say in your life, because people here don't want a lot of boring chit-chat. Come after you've had your kids and you are looking for a nice place to raise them; come after the kids are grown when you just want to spend a lot of time fussing in your garden. Come after you've earned your pile and are looking for some place to cultivate your "natural side."

It's not a coincidence that the roads in Vermont go nowhere. They were built for people who either have no need to travel and/or who have already traveled enough. You want to get to New York, you have to sneak along back roads and watch for tiny signs. You can't go across the state sideways because there is no need to. The only reason Interstate 89/91 was built was so that those damn fools who want to streak from Massachusetts to Canada would be kept carefully separated from the rest of the population. Quarantined as it were.

Let me give you an example. Deer. I once drove the length of New York state over Thanksgiving weekend. I saw 14 dead deer in 8 hours of driving. I have never seen a hit deer in Vermont after numerous runs up and down 89/91, meanderings to Bennington, Brattleburo, Burlington, Barre, Bread Loaf, Brookfield, Brownington, Bakersfield, Bridpoint, Birdland, Blissville, and Button Bay. Why? Because New York deer have a purpose; they have a vision. "Run across a busy road" is in their daily planners and they have to stick to their schedule. Their hoof-adapted PalmPilot will beep at them and remind them they are lagging behind in achieving their goals if they neglect road-crossing. New York deer aren't chicken; they don't ask WHY they have to cross. It's on the to-do list, so they do it. And occasionally they get hit.

Vermont deer have no agenda. They walk to the roadside. They look. They contemplate the tarmac. They sniff the wind; they meditate. They ask Mother Nature, their guru, the gods, the wind, Buddha, the universe, the spirits, ancestral deer, and/or draw a tarot card. Road crossing? Does it feel right? Does it seem appropriate? Would it be meaningful? Then they decide. Or don't decide. Or decide to decide later. Vermont deer don't have a timetable.

The deer are like snow. In Montana, the snow understands its purpose; it sees its function clearly. It is to fall from the heavens unto the earth. Quickly, and in no measly amount. Vermont snow ponders. It questions. It decides that, since it's falling anyway, might as well see a bit of the countryside before it settles. It visits other snowflakes. It goes horizontally. It comes in fits and bursts. A snow cloud will start and stop snowing six times in a day. I have seen it snow for eight hours and only have two inches of accumulation. I swear to you I have seen snow in Vermont going up.

And no one thinks anything of it. Far be it from a Vermonter to question, to complain. No, no. Vermonters are so understanding of such natural tendencies that they go ahead and use snow machines so the snow won't feel PRESSURED or anything to come down and behave like goal-oriented Montana snow. Vermonters who want a white Christmas will rent snow machines to make sure their front yards are white so as not to make recalcitrant, indecisive snow clouds from feeling guilty.

Come to Vermont when you are tired. Tired of being creative. Tired of having to remember things. Things like names. In Vermont, all 59 towns are derived from eleven basic names (informally known as the STN—Sacred Town Names). Thus you have Craftsbury, Craftsbury Common, East Craftsbury; Randolf, Randolf Center; Stowe, West Stowe, North Stowe, Old Stowe, Stowe Corners, etc.. Vermont is a place where people name their business after themselves (Mandy owns Mandy's Plumbing, Scott owns Scott's Lumber), the streets after themselves (George Smith lives on Smith Lane) and sometimes they even have the same name as their town. This seem a bit eerie to you? Ernestine lives on Ernestine Lane, in the town of Ernestine (or South Ernestine or West Ernestine) and works at Ernestine Cement. Cozy for a Vermonter but downright claustrophobic for normal folk.

Vermont is also for people who are tired of doing things. Things like putting up the Christmas decorations and taking down the Christmas decorations. In August, many is the house still decked out in Christmas regalia. And in Vermont, no need to take that pesky ski rack off during the summer months. Vermont is utterly forgiving of people who feel ski racks are like doors—an integral part of a car.

Right by the border with Massachusetts there should be a statue, not of a person, real Vermonters would not want a statue of themselves, but of a tree. And underneath the words: "Give us not your flat-landers, not your New Yorkers, give us only the meek, the quiet, the recyclers, yearning to live off the grid and pay a lot to throw garbage away."

CONCLUSION

ONCE AS I WAS PRAISING QUEEN ELIZABETH AS A ROLE-MODEL, A TROLL INTERRUPTED ME, "SHE WAS BORN RICH, HER LIFE IS EASY. She has nothing to do with me." Sigh. She has everything to do with you. Behaving well is not dependent on money, age, marital status or position in society.[1] It depends on self-control, attempting to put others at ease and understanding that your habits and customs are not universal. Behaving well seems easy: answer e-mails, say thank you, don't be late, only snark among close friends, but it's actually quite difficult, especially if you have decided to live overseas. Oh the legions of people who travel for new experiences and then get mad when the food is not what they are used to, nor is it ready at the 'right' time, nor is it served 'correctly' and people don't say what they mean and what are they wearing and why can't I find a decent... Of course, Darling, you have permission to grumble (especially in Malta!) but let's grumble with élan, with *joie de vivre*, with accurate and insightful comments. Let us make what beauty we can where we are, overpay staff, visit cafes, go after our dreams and behave well.

---

1. This book is for people who have enough money to be in control of their lives—refugees need to survive, not worry about the finer points of etiquette. But once you have crossed the threshold of having shelter, sufficient food, clean drinking water and enough income, then, Darling, you must pay heed.

ACKNOWLEDGMENTS

I would like to thank all my dear friends who had these essays hand-copied onto vellum with gold leaf capital letters which were then tied with archival-quality velvet ribbons and placed reverently in Vesuvius explosion/tidal wave/category 6 hurricane/tornado/Saskatchewan Screamer/Alberta Clipper/chomped by a Yeti/dropped from tall buildings-proof boxes and who begged me with teary faces and bended knee to have them printed.

ABOUT THE AUTHOR

L. M. Rainer is perfectly charming and always well behaved. These essays started as a way to pass on her extensive knowledge to her dearest niece, Esmeralda, but the writing rather got away from her and suddenly there were essays a go-go on every possible subject. Think of her as the Auntie Mame you never had, with a touch of Zena the Warrior Princess, Scout, Mary Queen of Scots, and Miss Piggy.

Find out more at https://howtobehave.net/

112 Harvard Ave #65
Claremont, CA 91711 USA

pelekinesis@gmail.com
www.pelekinesis.com
Pelekinesis titles are available through Small
Press Distribution, Ingram, Bertrams, and
directly from the publisher's website.

www.ingramcontent.com/pod-product-compliance
Lightning Source LLC
Chambersburg PA
CBHW010859090426
42738CB00019B/3450